# THE
# EVIDENCE
# FOR CREATION

### Examining the Origin of Planet Earth

## G.S. McLEAN
## ROGER OAKLAND
## LARRY McLEAN

# The Evidence for Creation

Glen McLean
Roger Oakland
Larry McLean

3rd Edition

Copyright © 1995 by Understand The Times
P O Box 27239
Santa Ana CA 92799
(714) 957-3898

Printed in the United States of America
ISBN: 0-9637797-1-0
Library of Congress Catalog Card Number: 95-60637

Scripture quotations marked *KJV* are taken from the *King James Version* of the Bible. Scripture quotations marked *NASB* are taken from the *New American Standard Bible, copyright* © 1960, 1962, 1963, 1968, 1971, 1972, 1973, 1975, 1977 by the Lockman Foundation. Used by permission.

# About The Book

The subject matter of this book is taken from a portion of a seminar series entitled *The Bible: Key To Understanding, Science, History and the Future* that was presented by the authors when they were traveling and speaking together as a team.

The book was first published under the title of *The Bible: Key To Understanding The Early Earth.* The second edition was published by Whitaker House under the title of *The Evidence For Creation: Examining The Origin Of Planet Earth.*

Although the book has been widely distributed in Canada and the United States, the greatest exposure for this book has been international in scope. It was the first book on the subject of creation to be published and printed in Russia. The availability of the book was announced over Russian National television the day after Gorbachev announced the collapse of the mighty Soviet Empire in December of 1991. To date over 300,000 copies of the Russian version are in circulation in Russia and other republics of the Commonwealth of Independent States. The book is also available in Spanish and is in the process of being translated into several other languages at the time of this printing.

The third edition of *The Evidence For Creation* is published by **Understand The Times,** a missionary organization founded by author and lecturer Roger Oakland.

# THE EVIDENCE FOR CREATION
# EXAMINING THE ORIGIN OF PLANET EARTH

# INTRODUCTION

The subject of the origin and history of life has always been a controversial issue. How did life originate? Was it the result of random chance processes over millions of years of time, or was it by a special plan of an almighty Creator-Designer who had a specific plan and purpose for the earth? These are questions that are often asked. Is it really possible to know the answers?

Over the past several years the controversy regarding the subject of origins has triggered heated debate between the two opposing views—creation and evolution. Even the courts have been called upon to try and decide whether or not creation could be taught alongside evolution in the public school system. Many individuals have rejected the creation model because it originates from the Bible, without even knowing or understanding the principles on which it is based.

The most popular model for the origin and history of life is the theory of evolution. This theory is widely upheld and accepted by the vast majority of scientists as the only logical explanation for the origin and history of life and the history of the earth. Most evolutionists would agree that because the theory of evolution is so well accepted, the theory is no longer a theory but a fact. Anyone who challenges the theory of evolution is often termed a religious kook or a fanatic. Evolutionists often meet opposition to their theory with outrage and emotional hostility.

Is it really possible to know which of these two models for origins is the correct one? Is there a test that can be made in order to examine the credibility of a theory? It is common knowledge that in order for a theory or a hypothesis to be classified as scientific, it must be supported by factual information. Any statement or idea that can not be backed up by sound, observable evidence should not come under the definition of science. The purpose of this book is to examine the creation and evolution models with this preceeding statement always in mind. The fundamental principles of both models will be examined in detail, then tested by looking at the actual observable evidence.

A number of excellent books have already been written by creationists which contain information similar to the material that will be covered in this book. The objective of presenting our material is not to duplicate something which has already been done. It is our desire that this book will simply and clearly present the two contrasting models for origins in such a way as to challenge the mind of any open-minded person. Wherever possible, diagrams, graphics, and photographs will be used to help illustrate important points to the reader. Part I will deal with the subject of the creation model. Part II will present the evolution model. Part III will cover the subject of the geological column and fossils and will be examined in the light of both models.

Another main objective we have in presenting this material is to confirm to the reader that the Bible, the Word of God, and the evidence from the world of God totally agree. However, simply presenting facts that confirm the authenticity of the Scriptures will in no way guarantee that someone opposed to the biblical model of origins will suddenly make a change of mind. A person who accepts the evolution premise as valid can not be convinced through intellectual reasoning that he is wrong. Only the Spirit of God can open the mind of one who is spiritually blind.

Over the past several years, thousands of committed evolutionists have considered the biblical premise of the origin and history of life and found it to be reasonable and true. It is our prayer that many others, even some that might read this book, will come to that same conclusion. The Bible, a book that can be the key to understanding the early earth and the history of life, is also the key to understanding the spiritual need of mankind. May God's Word and God's Spirit open to each heart a true understanding of the reality of our Lord and Savior, Jesus Christ.

# THE CREATION MODEL

"The fear of the Lord is the
beginning of knowledge . . ."

Proverbs 1:7

"The entrance of thy words
giveth light; it giveth
understanding unto the simple."

Psalms 119:130

# WHAT IS THE CREATION MODEL?

The creation model is claimed to be a revelation given to man by God the Creator describing various events that have transpired in the origin and history of the universe, the earth, and all living things that are found on the earth. The source of the creation model comes from the Bible, God's written revelation to man.

The Bible very clearly claims it is a book that has been written by the inspiration of God. Although the words have been penned by human hands, the source of the inspiration for the writing of the Bible, and thus the creation model, comes from God and God alone. Second Timothy 3:16 states:

*All Scripture is inspired by God and profitable for teaching, for reproof, for correction, for training in righteousness—NASB*

A creationist is a person who is willing to accept that the biblical account of origins and the history of the earth is acurate and reliable. A creationist also believes that the statements made in the Word of God should be able to be backed up and supported by physical evidence from the world that God has created. A creationist makes apology to no one that the Scriptures are used as a key for understanding the principle of origins and the history of the earth.

Very often a person who believes in the biblical model of creation is viewed by a nonbeliever as a naive, narrow-minded religious fanatic who is not willing to look at the observable evidence with an open mind. Because the evolutionary idea of origins has been so widely accepted by the scientific community, many people have reasoned that the creation model should be completely rejected without fairly examining its claims. Even many Christians who deeply reverence and trust the Bible have never really understood the claims of the creation account. One of the main objectives of this book is to discuss the major principles that the Bible reveals regarding creation, backing up each statement with sound, observable evidence. Over the past several years, a great deal of controversy surrounding the creation-evolution issue has been generated by degreed scientists who have based their claims on the creation model and have been willing to let their reputations stand. Creationists have openly requested that when the discussion of origins occurs in the public school system, both the model of creation and evolution be presented side by side.

Initially, scientists and educators who have accepted the theory of evolution without question were reluctant to pay any serious attention to creationism. However, it now has become apparent that substantial numbers of people are taking creationism seriously. Many evolutionists view this trend as a serious threat to the advancement of science and have vowed to do everything in their power to stop the teaching of creation in the public school system. Most evolutionists now view creationism as nothing more than a particular version of fundamental Christianity with no valid scientific content.

The best way to examine the creation model is to study each of its claims. The creation model consists of a number of fundamental principles. In order to better understand the biblical account of creation, let's look at each of these claims in detail, showing how each can be supported by logical and sound, observable evidence.

# GOD—THE CREATOR

The very first verse of the Bible contains the most important principle of the creation model. Genesis 1:1 states: "In the beginning God . . ." The biblical concept of origins is centered around the existence of an all-powerful, eternal Designer who had a definite plan and purpose for His creation. The universe, the solar system, our planet earth, and all living things came into existence by the plan and design of a super-intelligent, creative being.

Over the past several centuries, scientific research has accumulated an incredible amount of information about the design that exists in the universe and the immediate world around us. Many intelligent men and woman devote their entire lives to the study of the chemical and physical laws of nature, as well as observing the structure and function of the components and systems which make up living things. These amazing discoveries that are made by scientists reveal the existence of a complexity that is beyond the scope of human understanding. Where did this design and complexity come from?

Every one of us has had thoughts and questions regarding the origin of design. Logic and experience have shown us that any object we see in the world around us which exhibits design could not have arisen by some spontaneous process. For example, a book is the product of many hours of careful planning and writing by an author. Paintings are the product of an idea or a scene visualized by an artist. Then the image is skillfully transferred to a canvas using a brush guided by a human hand. Buildings are designed by architects who draw blueprints that various tradesmen can use to assemble complex sructures in an orderly way.

The universe around us reveals complexity and design that staggers our imagination. Atoms, molecules, cells, and all living things clearly show the evidence of a master plan and the design of an intelligent being. Logic further confirms that design demands a designer. Does it not seem reasonable, therefore, to accept that the complexity and design we observe in the universe is the product of an intelligent Creator-Designer? The very first premise that is presented by the creation model is sound, logical, and true.

*Figure 1:*
*The atom is the basic building block of every physical thing in the universe. Its basic components are space, matter, and energy.*

# THE BUILDING BLOCKS OF CREATION

In order to begin any kind of building project, the manufacturer or designer must first assemble the raw materials. For example, if you were to engineer the construction of a building, various kinds of essential construction materials such as wood, cement, and bricks would have to be first located at the building site. It is interesting that the biblical account of creation begins by giving a detailed explanation of the raw materials or building blocks that were assembled for the construction of the universe.

We know everything that exists in the universe is made up of building blocks called atoms. The atom consists of three basic components: space, matter, and energy. *(Figure 1.)* These three basic components of the atom are the first things that God brought into existence during the first day of creation, and are mentioned in the first three verses of Scripture.

## Space and Matter

Genesis 1:1-3 states:

> *In the beginning God created the heaven and the earth. And the earth was without form, and void; and darkness was upon the face of the deep. And the Spirit of God moved upon the face of the waters. And God said, Let there be light: and there was light.*

Examining these verses in detail will give us a better understanding of the initial stages of the creation process. For example, verse one mentions God created the *heaven* and the *earth.* As we examine this passage, it suggests to us God created the heavenly bodies in the universe as well as our planet earth. However, when we study the actual meaning of the words *heaven* and *earth* from the Hebrew context in which Genesis was originally written, we find these two words have a broader meaning.

The word *heaven* that is translated in verse one is the Hebrew word *shamayim*, which means heavens, or a stretched out expanse, or *space*. One of the first things God did was to bring space into being. Secondly, the word *earth* is the Hebrew word *erets*, which can mean, earth, dirt, land, matter, or the substance from which things are formed. Thus, according to the Word of God, creation begins by two major components of the atom being brought into existence — *space and matter.*

## Without Form and Void

A second important aspect of the creation of the building blocks is stated in Scripture. The *earth* or *matter* was "without form, and void" (Genesis 1:2). That phrase simply means that matter had not been put into any meaningful form or design at that time.

The randomness referred to as "without form, and void" can be illustrated by taking a child's container of building blocks and tossing them in a pile on the floor. The blocks would obviously show no constructive order. *(Figure 2.)* In the same way matter, which is one of the basic components of atomic structure, had not been organized into any meaningful form or design.

## Light

The third major component of atomic structure is light. Scripture states: "And God said, Let there be light" (Genesis 1:3). When God brought light into existence, He created the whole electromagnetic spectrum. *(Figure 3.)* Often we think of light as being only visible light that can be observed with our eyes. However, a closer examination of the definition of

*Figure 2:*
*The building blocks above are "without form, and void."*
*Below, the building blocks have been arranged into a*
*meaningful form.*

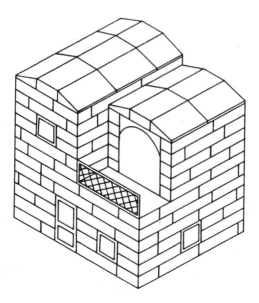

light reveals it includes frequencies from a much broader spectrum that can not be visually perceived.

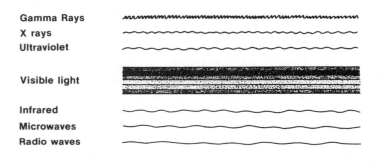

*Figure 3:*
*The electromagnetic spectrum is made up of many different wave lengths of light energy.*

Each wavelength in the electromagnetic spectrum from gamma rays to radio waves carries a different amount of energy. Only light, the wavelengths that make up the band of the colors of the rainbow, is visible to the human eye.

Thus, when God said, "Let there be light," the whole electromagnetic spectrum came into existence. In other words, *energy* came into being. When the energy contained within the atom is measured, we find it falls within the boundaries of the electromagnetic spectrum.

As we have seen, the first three verses of Scripture give us a clear understanding of the origin of space, matter, and energy, which are the three basic components of the atom, the building blocks of the universe. *(Figure 4.)* Isn't it interesting that the Bible gives an accurate description of the components of an atom as we understand it today?

HEAVENS = SPACE
EARTH = MATTER
LIGHT = ENERGY

*Figure 4:*
*The components of the atom were brought into existence on the first day of creation.*

## The Significance of Water

Another very important feature mentioned in the first few verses of Scripture deals with the subject of water. Genesis 1:2 states: "the Spirit of God moved upon the face of the waters." Apparently God's Spirit did something special or unique with water.

What evidence is there to indicate that water is a unique substance? Our immediate observation would indicate water is one of the most common compounds found on the surface of our planet. Over two-thirds of the surface of the earth is covered with water.

A close examination of the properties of water show it is a very unique and complex substance. It is one of the few compounds which does not follow the natural laws of chemistry. Instead of contracting when it is frozen, water expands to create ice. *(Figure 5.)* This solid form of water is lighter than the liquid form, which is a very important factor for all life forms that live under water in cold climatic conditions. If water did not have this property, lakes and rivers would freeze from the bottom up, causing organisms living underwater to perish.

Water plays an important role in regulating the earth's temperature. Water vapor in the earth's atmosphere helps to shield the surface from intense heat radiated by the sun in the daytime. At night, the water vapor acts as a canopy and prevents the loss of heat by radiating back to space. Another important factor to the regulation of the earth's climate is that water can absorb a great deal of heat before its temperature is raised very much. Heat can then be lost by evaporation of

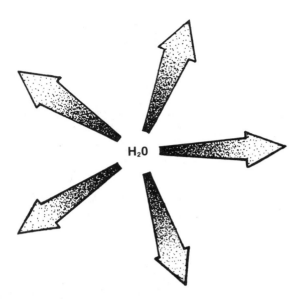

*Figure 5:*
*Most substances contract as they cool.*
*In contrast, water expands as it freezes into a solid form.*

small amounts of water, which tends to bring about a moderation of the earth's temperature.

Water is absolutely essential for the existence of life. Space probes, searching for life that might exist in other parts of our solar system, look for the presence of water. The major portion of every living thing is made up of water, which it requires for its continued survival. Of all known liquids it is the best solvent, as more substances can be dissolved in it than in anything else. There is no question that water is a very unique substance. Isn't it interesting that the Spirit of God did something special to water on the very first day of creation?

# THE CREATION DAY

The biblical account of origins very clearly states the creation took place over a period of six days. What does the Bible mean by a day of creation? Is this a day of normal duration as we would understand a day, or does it refer to a longer period of time? Many biblical scholars have suggested that a day of creation refers to millions of years of geological time. Some even suggest God used the process of evolution to bring about the creation of all life forms. In this way they attempt to compromise for the billions of years of time proposed by the geological time.

## The Day-Age Theory

A popular theory that has attempted to harmonize a creation day with long periods of geological time and therefore be compatible with the idea of evolution is the day-age theory. Those who hold this view believe there is a correspondence between the order of geological history, as outlined by the evolutionary theory, and the order of creation as stated in the Bible. However, a close examination of the Scriptures indicates the two views do not agree. Let's look at several reasons why this concept is not compatible with a literal interpretation of the Bible.

1. The Bible states all plant life came into existence on the third day of creation, but fish and marine organisms were created on the fifth day. The geological theory for the origin and progression of life reverses this order.

2. The Bible states God made the sun, moon, and stars on the fourth day of creation. This is the day following the creation of the plant kingdom. Obviously, vegetation could not exist for long periods of time without sunlight, therefore the suggestion that a day of creation could be equivalent to millions of years would not be possible.

3. The Bible states the birds were created on the same day as fish and other marine organisms. Geological theory maintains that birds evolved from reptiles at a period of time millions of years after the time period when fish first appeared.

4. The Bible indicates insects were among the last things created, coming on the scene at the same time as land animals and reptiles. According to evolutionary geology, insects appeared early in the geological record preceding the appearance of reptiles and land animals.

Reading through the first chapter of Genesis, we see that each creation day is bounded by a morning and an evening. This is the same terminology we would use to describe a normal day. Thus it would appear that each creation day is a literal day or a day of normal duration.

God further clarifies the length of a creation day. In Exodus 20:8-11, God makes the following statement while giving the Ten Commandments to the children of Israel:

*Remember the sabbath day, to keep it holy. Six days shalt thou labour, and do all thy work: but the seventh day is the sabbath of the Lord thy God: in it thou shalt not do any work . . . For in six days the Lord made heaven and earth, the sea, and all that in them is, and rested on the seventh day: wherefore the Lord blessed the sabbath day, and hallowed it.*

From these verses we see God told man that he should work for six days, then take a day of rest. God compared these days to the days of the creation week. From the context of the scripture, it is obvious the length of the days of the creation week are compared with days of normal duration and can not be equated to thousands or millions of years of time.

A further objection to the day-age theory and the idea life could be created by the process of evolution involves the problem of trying to explain the existence of death prior to the curse or the fall. Obviously, if millions of years of time were involved in the development of life in an evolutionary process, death would occur over and over again. The theory of evolution on which the geological time scale is based suggests death is a natural phenomenon which has occurred from the moment life began. The whole concept of evolution is based on the suggestion that disease and death work in a process of natural selection, which ultimately brings about the existence of man. The Bible makes it very clear that death entered this world through Adam's sin. Romans 5:12 states:

> *Therefore, just as through one man sin entered into the world, and death through sin, and so death spread to all men, because all sinned—NASB.*

We can conclude that the only reasonable explanation for the time period of the creation week is a literal one. Creation took place in six literal days. The Scriptures tell us God rested after the sixth day when creation was completed. The processes used by God in this creative act are no longer in action and therefore can not be studied in terms of the various physical laws as we understand them today.

# WHEN DID CREATION TAKE PLACE?

When did it all begin? How old is the earth? Did the earth originate millions and millions of years ago in the past or was it something that happened perhaps in recent historical times?

The subject of the age of the earth has always been a controversial issue. No human being was there in the beginning to make first hand observations. As a result, man's speculation on the subject of the age of the earth has brought about a number of different views.

The evolutionary viewpoint claims the earth is very old. The majority of scientific sources dealing with this subject state that the universe is between 15 and 20 billion years old and that the earth is about 4.5 to 5 billion years old.

*Figure 6:*
*The age of the universe is a controversial issue that interests everyone. Can scientists know for certain just how old the universe really is? (Front cover of the March 12, 1995* **Time)**

As will be mentioned later in this book, the billions of years of time necessary for the evolutionary world view was first established by geologists in the 1700's. It was proposed that the layers of the earth, called strata, had been formed gradually over millions of years of time.

*Figure 7:*
*An aerial view of a portion of "The Little Grand Canyon "which was rapidly formed just north of the Mount St. Helens volcano by a mud flow on March 19, 1982. The canyon wall reveals layers that have been formed catastrophically (see Figure 8)*

Creationists who believe in the Biblical account of origins can be divided into two separate camps when it comes to the subject of the age of the earth. Old earth creationists agree with the evolutionary world view that the layers of the earth required millions of years of time to be laid down. In order to accommodate the long periods of time necessary for this view, the old earth creationists believe the Biblical creation days were not actually days, but instead were periods of time representing millions of years.

Young earth creationists believe the layers of the earth were formed catastrophically during a short time period when the earth was severely devastated at the time of Noah's flood. Young earth creationists take the position that the creation days were literal days as we would understand a day today. Although it can not be stated dogmatically, the Biblical account of the genealogies, or the records of the generations since Adam as listed in scripture, seem to indicate that the

*Figure 8:*
*Fine layering was produced within hours at Mount St. Helens on June 12, 1980, by hurricane-velocity surging flows from the crater of the volcano. The twenty-five-foot-thick, June 12 deposit is exposed in the middle of the cliff. It is overlain by the massive, but thinner, March 19, 1982, mudflow deposit, and is underlain by the air-fall debris from the last hours of the May 18, 1980, nine-hour eruption. (Photo by Steven A. Austin. Used by permission. Copyright Institute for Creation Research.)*

Creation week took place only thousands of years ago.

The suggestion of such a young age for the earth to people who have accepted the evolutionary model of the earth's history is absolutely ridiculous. Obviously there is a very large difference between five billion and only a few thousand years. If one is correct, then the other must be seriously in error.

It is interesting that many people have established their view on the age of the earth without examining the evidence for themselves. As well, the evolutionary assumption that very long periods of time were necessary for the formation of the earth's layers is a concept that needs to be reevaluated in light of current information. For example, geologists have witnessed the formation of layers on the earth's surface by catastrophic events involving only a few moments of time as demonstrated by the Mount St. Helen's eruptions of 1980 and 1983. Certainly layers of the earth do not take millions of years to form. They can be formed very quickly. (See figures 7 and 8.)

## Geochronology

The science of geochronology deals with the subject of determining the age of the earth. At present there are over eighty different methods which are used in an attempt to date the earth. Most people are unaware that the majority of these methods give a young age for the earth and not the proposed billions of years as strongly upheld by the evolutionists. (Figure 9.) Later in this book when we discuss the evolution model in more detail, we will see why this concept of long periods of time is so essential for the feasibility of the evolutionary theory.

Young earth creationists believe the age of the earth is much younger than the evolutionary timetable suggests. In their attempt to support this view, they point to the study of geo-

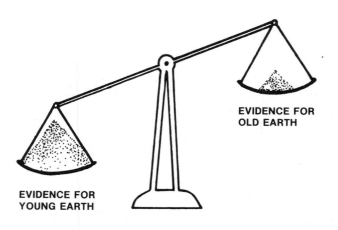

*Figure 9:*
*The majority of the methods for determining the age of the earth*
*indicate the earth is young. Only a few questionable methods of*
*geochronology support the evolutionary concept of billions of years*
*of age*

chronology. However, it is important to note that geochronology is based on the assumption that things are occurring
today at the same rate that they did in the past. This concept
is also the basis of uniformitarianism which is the belief that
the various factors such as erosion by wind and water, volcanic activity and the rising and sinking of land are occurring
today at the same rate as they did in the past. These assumptions can not be verified.

There have been a number of books written which docu-
ment the evidence supporting a young earth. *"The Young*
*Earth"*, by Dr. John Morris, published by Master Books, is an
excellent book in this regard. For our purposes, we will look
at a few examples which seem to indicate the earth may well
be much younger than evolution claims.

# Earth's Magnetic Field

One method of geochronology that shows a young age for the earth is the measurement of the strength of the earth's magnetic field. Analysis of data recorded over the past 130 years indicates the strength of the magnetic field has been getting weaker and weaker.

If we were to draw a graph using the data that has been collected, and making the assumption that the rate of magnetic decay has been the same in the past as it is today, the strength of the earth's magnetic field would have been equivalent to a magnetic star only 10,000 years ago. (Figure 10.)

Obviously, no life could possibly exist under these conditions. If the graph was extrapolated back as far as 30,000 years, then the magnetic strength of the earth would have been sufficient enough to generate temperatures in excess of 5000 degrees C. This temperature is sufficient enough to melt or vaporize the elements of the earth. According to this method of geochronology, there is evidence to show the earth can not be as old as suggested by the evolution model.

Another important factor that must be considered as a result of the earth's decreased magnetic field is the effect this condition would have on the Van Allen radiation belts that surround the earth. (Figure 11.) These belts are very important in determining how much cosmic radiation reaches the surface of the earth. Cosmic radiation in turn is an important factor in determining the rate of radioactive carbon 14 formation.

Carbon 14 is a method used for dating organic material and is based on the assumption that the amount of radioactive carbon in the earth's atmosphere has always been constant. If

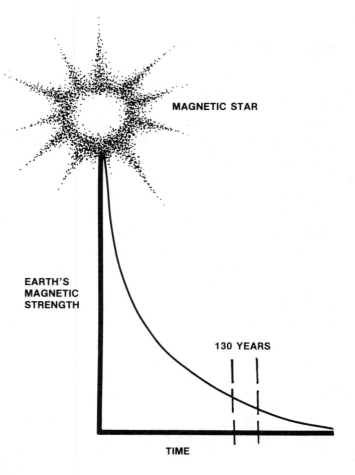

MAGNETIC STAR

EARTH'S
MAGNETIC
STRENGTH

130 YEARS

TIME

*Figure 10:*
*The earth's magnetic strength is decreasing with time. Measurements over the past 130 years recorded a 14 percent decrease, indicating the earth's magnetic strength decays by one-half every 1400 years. If this decay has remained constant, 10,000 years ago the earth's magnetic strength would have been equivalent to that of a magnetic star. No life could have survived on earth with magnetism of that intensity.*

there has been any fluctuation in the earth's magnetic field in the past, then the accuracy of the carbon 14 method would be highly suspect. We will discuss this area in more detail when we look at the subject of radiometric dating.

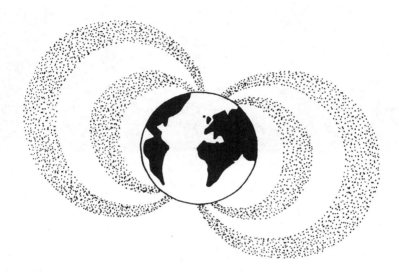

*Figure 11:*
*The strength of the Van Allen radiation belts around the earth is dependent upon the strength of the earth's magnetic field. If the earth's magnetic strength has been decreasing over time, the Van Allen radiation belts have not remained constant. This important factor poses serious questions concerning the reliability of the carbon 14 dating method.*

## Erosion of Continents

The erosional processes of wind and water provide another important factor indicating a young age for the earth. (Figure 12.)

*Figure 12:*
*The present rate of wind and water erosion would erode*
*continents to sea level within 14 million years.*

Given the present rate of erosion, the continents could be completely eroded to sea level within 14 million years. Although 14 million years is a lot longer than the age of the earth proposed by the creation model, it is less than one-half of one percent of the age proposed by the evolution model.

## Oil and Gas Deposits

Another interesting observation supporting the concept of a young earth pertains to the extremely high pressures associated with oil and gas deposits beneath the earth's surface. *(Figure 13.)* Many of these deposits are surrounded by porous material that would allow the dissipation of high pressures over the millions of years of time. The high pressure that remains gives a clear indication that petroleum deposits can not possibly be as old as theory suggests.

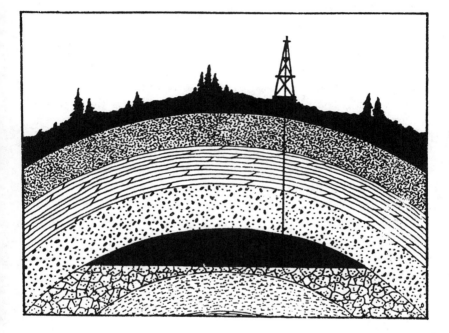

*Figure 13:*
*Oil and natural gas are found in deposits of porous rock and*
*sand. The extremely high pressure found in many of these*
*porous reservoirs would have dissipated by now if these*
*deposits were more than 10,000 to 100,000 years old.*

These are just a few of the methods of geochronology used to lend proof to the idea that the earth is young. Certainly there is adequate evidence to challenge preconceived ideas that the earth and the universe are billions of years old.

## Evidence for an Old Earth

There are a number of methods used in the science of geochronology that seem to indicate an extreme age for the earth. This of course fits with the evolutionary concept. These methods we will be looking at are referred to as the *radiometric dating methods*. Most scientists are convinced these dating techniques are accurate and reliable. It is very common to read scientific publications which have used radiometric methods for dating certain layers of the earth. Radiometric dating methods have become an important basis for the claim that the earth is billions of years old.

Let us consider how the radiometric dating methods measure time. The most common methods that are used are:

1. Uranium-lead method
2. Rubidium-strontium method
3. Potassium-argon method

In each of these systems the parent element, or the element which is undergoing decay (uranium, rubidium, potassium), is gradually changed into the daughter component (lead, strontium, argon) of the system. With the use of an instrument called a mass spectrometer, it is possible to measure the ratio of the parent and daughter elements involved. The radiometric decay rate of the system is then used to determine how long the process of decay has been taking place.

The radiometric dating techniques are based on three assumptions:

1. The system must have been initially made up of all parent elements and no daughter elements.
2. The rate of decay must have been constant from the moment the process was started.

3. The system must operate as a closed system. Nothing from the system can be taken away; nothing from outside the system can be added.

As we examine these basic assumptions, the highly speculative nature of the radiometric dating methods becomes apparent. None of these assumptions are testable or provable, and therefore not scientific. For example it is impossible for anyone to know the initial components of the system. To state that the system began as 100% parent element and 0% daughter element is an outright guess. Secondly, it is unreasonable to suggest the decay rate has always taken place in the past at the same rate it is observed today. Every process in nature operates at a rate influenced by numerous environmental factors. In the process of radiometric decay, for example, extreme temperature change alters the rate very significantly. Thirdly, there is no such thing as a closed system in nature. The whole concept of having a process taking place over long periods without any outside interference is purely hypothetical. It is totally impossible to make the claim that parent or daughter elements have neither been added to nor taken away from the system over millions of years of time.

In order to better understand how these dating techniques work, let's look at some different examples. If a scientist wants to determine the age of a specific rock or layer; what procedure would he use? One of the common materials that is used in dating procedures is rock which originates from volcanic activity. *(Figure 14.)* Often fossils are found in layers surrounded by volcanic material. In order to determine the age of the fossil, an age is assigned to the volcanic material that is either above, below, or around it by using the potassium-argon or uranium-lead radiometric techniques. Often these dates are published in scientific journals and accepted as accurate and reliable.

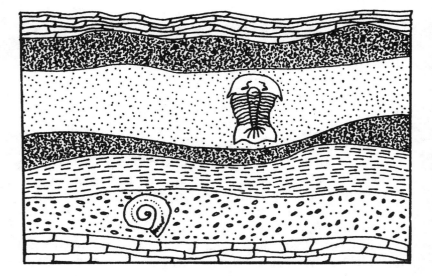

*Figure 14:*
*In order to determine the age of a fossil, volcanic materials from layers surrounding the fossil are subjected to radiometric dating. Are these techniques reliable?*

## How Reliable Are Radiometric Dates?

How reliable are these dating methods? We have already seen that the theory behind the dating procedure is based on several assumptions that can not be tested. Is there other evidence to indicate there are reasonable grounds for questioning these procedures? There are numerous examples of inconsistencies that raise serious doubts about the validity of radiometric dating. Let's look at some of these examples. Lunar soil obtained from the Apollo 11 mission was dated by four different radiometric methods. The results from these dating procedures produced four different ages.

$$Pb207\text{-}Pb206 \quad - \quad 4.6 \text{ billion years}$$
$$Pb206\text{-}U238 \quad - \quad 5.41 \text{ billion years}$$
$$Pb207\text{-}U235 \quad - \quad 4.89 \text{ billion years}$$
$$Pb208\text{-}Th232 \quad - \quad 8.20 \text{ billion years}$$

Lunar rocks taken from the same location and dated by a potassium-argon dating technique gave an age of 2.3 billion years. Five different dates were determined by five different methods. Which one of these dates is the correct one, or are any of them correct? These findings were reported in *Science*, volume 167, January 30, 1970.

The Apollo 16 mission brought back a moon rock that was dated by three different methods giving ages ranging from 7 to 18 billion years old. Research scientists determined these ages were not correct because of an excess of lead in the samples. Removal of the lead by an acid treatment produced an age of 3.8 billion years which was considered acceptable. This was reported in *Science*, volume 182, January 30, 1973, page 916.

If there is an uncertainty about the accuracy of a dating technique, a good way of testing the method would be dating a material of a known age. If the dating procedure came up with the same age as the known material, then you would know the method was accurate and reliable. Let's look at what happens when volcanic material of a known age is tested by radiometric techniques. *The Journal of Geophysical Research,* volume 73, July 15, 1968, reported that lava rocks that were formed underwater in 1800 and 1801 in Hawaii and dated by a potassium-argon method showed an age of formation of 160 million to 3 billion years. This shows a tremendous discrepancy between the actual age of formation and the age determined by a radiometric method.

There are numerous other examples in the scientific literature that show that when volcanic rocks of recent formation are dated, they give ages of formation at hundreds of millions to billions of years old. It is apparent the reliability of these dating methods is in question and is certainly not as accurate as we have been told. We must remember these same dating techniques are the ones scientists believe give verification for the earth and its layers being billions of years old.

Most of us have read articles in scientific publications that give precise dates for important finds supporting the evolutionary view of origins. Most readers rely heavily on the accuracy of these dates and accept them without question. Let's look at some examples to show how some of these dates are determined.

*National Geographic,* June, 1973, has a very important article called "Skull 1470," telling about a humanlike skull found by Richard Leakey in Africa. (Figure 15.) The reader is told the skull was determined to be 2.8 million years old. The article states the date was determined by the use of the potassium-argon radiometric dating procedure by dating volcanic material in which the skull was found.

Another interesting article is found in *National Geographic,* December, 1976. Here we are told about some important skeletal remains found by Donald Carl Johanson. (Figure 16.) Johanson, who has nicknamed his discovery "Lucy," claims this organism is a credible link in the proposed lineage from ape to man. The article makes the claim that the age of this specimen is approximately 3 million years old. The age was determined by doing a potassium-argon test using volcanic materials in the layers surrounding the fossil.

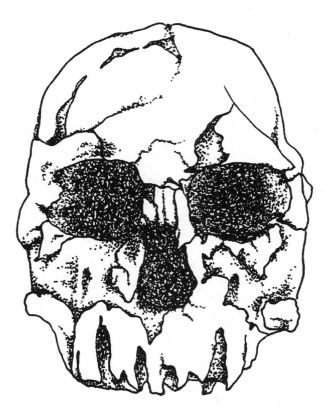

*Figure 15:*
*Skull 1470, found by Richard Leakey, is claimed to be 2.8 million years old. National Geographic, June 1973, page 824, states: "layers of volcanic tuff, datable by the potassium-argon method have led scientists to fix the age of the level that yielded the '1470' skull at 2.8 million years." Note: volcanic material was used to determine this age.*

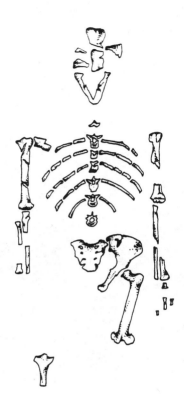

*Figure 16:*
*"Lucy," a skelton found by Donald Carl Johnson, is alleged to be three million years old. National Geographic, December 1976, page 801, indicates that volcanic tuff dated by the potassium-argon method "determines the dates of volcanic eruptions, thus placing age limits on fossils deposited above and below." Note: **volcanic material** is used to determine age.*

Or we could look at an article called "Footprints in the Ashes of Time," by Mary Leakey, as reported in *National Geographic,* April, 1979. These footprints are claimed to be made by ape-like humans living 3.6 million years ago. Once again, we are told dating was accomplished by the use of the potassium-argon method on volcanic material.

Prior to these three examples, we discussed the high degree of inaccuracy exhibited in dating volcanic material of a known age. We saw how volcanic material formed on the surface of the earth as recently as 200 years ago gave an age of millions of years by radiometric methods. In light of this kind of evidence we must question the reliability of the radiometric dating methods.

## Carbon 14 Dating

The radiometric methods that we previously discussed deal with measuring the age of materials classified as inorganic or non-living material. Now we are going to look at a dating method commonly used for dating organic material, or material which at one time was part of a living organism.

The carbon 14 method is based upon the measurement of the radioactive element, carbon 14, found in all living tissues. As a result of radiation passing through the upper atmosphere of the earth, ordinary nitrogen atoms are changed into radioactive carbon 14. *(Figure 17.)* Some of these radioactive atoms are then incorporated into carbon dioxide molecules which are in turn taken up by plants in the process of photosynthesis. Animals consume plant material or meat that can be traced back to a plant source. Thus every living organism, whether plant or animal, contains a certain amount of radioactive carbon 14.

When an organism dies, carbon 14 intake ceases, and the radioactive element begins the process of decay back to nitrogen. By measuring the amount of radioactive carbon in a sample, an indication can be made as to date of death. The more carbon 14 present, the younger the age; the less there is, the older the specimen.

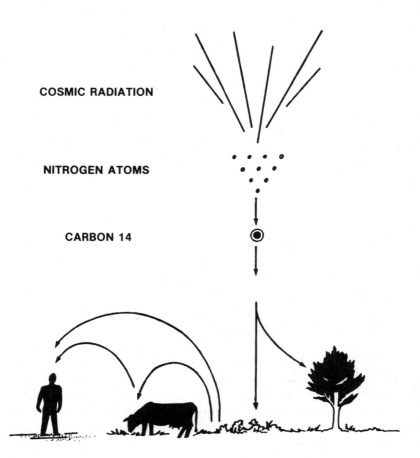

*Figure 17:*
*Cosmic radiation produces radioactive carbon 14, which eventually becomes a component of all living things.*

As with other radiometric dating methods, the carbon 14 method depends on several important assumptions. First, in order for this method of dating to work, the amount of radioactive carbon in the earth's atmosphere must have been constant. This would mean the rate of formation of radioactive carbon would have had to equal the decay rate in the age which the specimens lived. Second, it must be assumed the decay rate was the same in the past as it is today. Third, no contamination of radioactive carbon could occur since the death of the specimen.

In order to fairly evaluate the accuracy of the carbon 14 dating method, let's examine the observable evidence. There are a number of environmental factors that we could look at which indicate that the rate of radioactive carbon formation has not been constant in the past.

1. The power of the earth's magnetic field has decreased by approximately 14 percent over the past 130 years. As a result of the decreasing magnetic field, cosmic radiation more readily penetrates the earth's atmosphere, thus increasing the rate of carbon 14 formation. This observation indicates the rate of formation has not been constant in the past. *(Figure 18.)*

2. Volcanic activity in the past would also be an important factor. One of the major components of a volcanic eruption is the liberation of carbon dioxide. Periods of violent volcanic eruptions would upset the carbon 14 balance required for this method to be valid.

3. Solar flare activity taking place on the sun is responsible for an increased rate of formation of radioactive carbon.

4. Nuclear tests made in the past several decades have been responsible for an increase in the rate of radioactive carbon formation.

5. Collisions of asteroids or meteorites taking place on the earth are responsible for drastically increasing the rate of radioactive carbon formation. For example, the Tunguska

explosion in Siberia in 1908, which was attributed to an asteroid or a meteorite exploding in the earth's atmosphere, caused such an increase. Tree rings from all over the world indicate that the measurement of radioactivity was much greater than normal the year following the Siberian explosion.

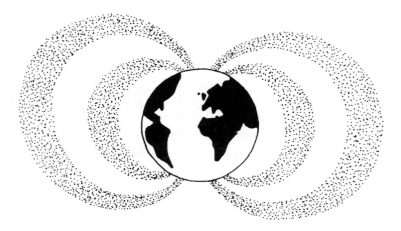

*Figure 18:*
*The strength of the Van Allen radiation belts affects the amount of cosmic radiation entering the earth's atmosphere to produce carbon 14. As the earth's magnetic field decays over time, the Van Allen belts weaken, allowing more cosmic radiation to penetrate the atmosphere. The rate of carbon 14 formation has not been constant.*

It is inaccurate to assume the rate of carbon 14 formation and decay to have been constant in the past. There is no possible way of making adjustments to compensate for all the variables that have occurred in the past. A fair evaluation of the observable evidence clearly indicates that carbon 14 dating is highly suspect.

## Reliability Of Carbon 14 Dating

How reliable is the carbon 14 radioactive dating method? When dates are published in various scientific articles, can we accept these as being accurate and unquestionable? Many scientists have claimed the dating of organic material is trustworthy and precise as a Swiss watch. Let's look at a few examples indicating good reason to question the reliability of this method.

1. Living mollusks have been dated by the carbon 14 procedure and assigned an age of 2300 years old. These results were recorded in *Science,* volume 130, December 11, 1959.
2. *Nature,* volume 225, March 7, 1970, reported a carbon 14 test was done on organic material contained in the mortar of an English castle. Although the castle was known to be 787 years old, the carbon 14 date gave an age of 7370 years old.
3. Freshly killed seals were dated by the carbon 14 method and an age was assigned at 1300 years old; Mummified seals that had been dead for thirty years dated 4600 years old. These results were reported in the *Antarctic Journal of the United States,* volume 6, 1971.

The following chart illustrates a sampling of dates taken from the scientific journals *Radiocarbon* and *Science.* It gives a comparison of carbon 14 dates with dating of specimens by the geological time frame. The geological dates or ages were determined by evolutionists well over 100 years ago, and are still acknowledged by the majority of scientists today as accurate and reasonable.

| Sample | Carbon 14 Date | Geological Date |
|---|---|---|
| sabre tooth tiger | 28,000 | 100,000—1,000,000 |
| mammoth | 11,000 | 20,000—35,000 |
| natural gas | 14,000 | 50,000,000 |
| coal | 1,680 | 100,000,000 |

It is obvious there is a very large discrepancy between the carbon 14 dates and the dates proposed by the geological column. However, both these dating methods are accepted as accurate and dependable by those who support the evolutionary theory, even though one obviously contradicts the other.

As we have examined the observable evidence regarding the question of the age of the earth, we have seen there are sufficient grounds to support the concept for a young earth. As we have seen, the majority of methods of geochronology indicate the earth is young. The radiometric techniques for dating the fossils and layers of the earth are not as reliable as we have been told. Obviously you do not have to be classified as a religious kook or fanatic if you hold to the biblical concept of a young earth. According to the creation model the earth is young. The observable evidence agrees.

# THE CANOPIED EARTH

The Bible indicates that the original earth was very much different from the earth as we know it today. *(Figure 19.)* One of the important features mentioned is the presence of an envelope or layer of water surrounding the earth. Genesis 1:6-7 states:

> *And God said, Let there be a firmament in the midst of the waters, and let it divide the waters from the waters. And God made the firmament, and divided the waters which were under the firmament from the waters which were above the firmament: and it was so.*

Examining these two verses in more detail will help give us a better understanding of what the Bible tells us the original earth was like. We are told that a *firmament* divided a layer of water that was above from a layer of water below. *(Figure 20.)* The word *firmament* is referring to the atmospheric layer surrounding the earth. The Scriptures clarify this in verse 20 by stating:

> *Let the waters bring forth abundantly the moving creature that hath life, and fowl that may fly above the earth in the open firmament of heaven.*

The condition described to us in these two verses could best be illustrated as a ball of water surrounding the earth. As a result of this unique situation, the earth would be protected by a canopy of water which would produce a subtropical greenhouse effect.

## The Greenhouse Effect

The presence of a layer of water surrounding the original

*Figure 19:*
*According to the Bible, the original earth was surrounded by*
*a layer of water. This diagram illustrates what the canopied*
*earth may have looked like from a viewpoint in outer space.*
*A section of the canopy has been removed to show the three*
*dimensional perspective.*

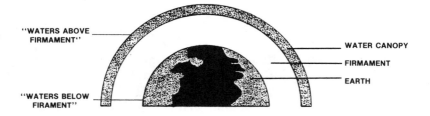

*Figure 20:*
*A sectional view of the canopied earth illustrates the separa-*
*tion of the earth from the watery layer of a firmament.*

earth would produce a number of environmental factors very different from what our present earth experiences. In order to better understand the canopy model, let's examine some of the features that a layer of water around the earth would produce.

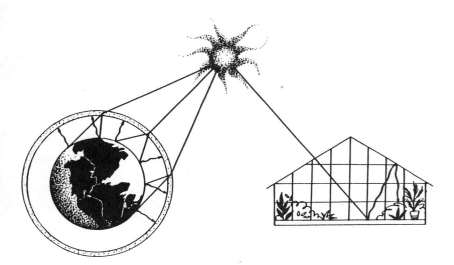

*Figure 21:*
*The presence of a water canopy surrounding the original earth would have provided a greenhouse effect. Long wave radiation from the sun would pass through the water canopy and be scattered in many different directions. Radiated heat from the earth's surface in the form of short wave radiation would be trapped inside the canopy, creating conditions similar to the environment produced in a greenhouse. Subtropical environment conditions would have existed from pole to pole.*

Sunlight, or long wave radiation, would pass through the layer of water in the upper atmosphere and be diffused and scattered in many different directions. Light would reach all latitudes with an equal intensity. Radiated heat from the earth's surface in the form of short wave radiation would be trapped inside the watery canopy. This would produce a greenhouse-type environment over the entire surface of the globe. As a result, there would be a subtropical climate from pole to pole. Subtropical plant and animal life would exist over the entire surface of the earth. *(Figure 21.)*

The canopy surrounding the earth would produce a very stable climate. There would not be extreme climatic differences like those we experience today as a result of unequal heating of the earth's surface. Under present atmospheric conditions, sunlight strikes the earth more directly at the equator than it does at the polar regions. This condition causes it to be hotter at the equator and cooler towards the polar regions. *(Figure 22.)*

Differentiation of temperatures around the globe produces differences in atmospheric pressures, which in turn results in the production of winds. As winds move back and forth across the globe attempting to balance differences in pressure, precipitation results when cold and warm air masses meet.

Because of the uniform temperatures produced by a canopy, the original earth would have had very humid, moist conditions but there would not have been any rain. It is interesting that the Bible states in Genesis 2:5-6: ''The Lord God had not caused it to rain upon the earth, and there was not a man to till the ground. But there went up a mist from the earth, and watered the whole face of the ground.'' According to the biblical model there was no rain before the time of the flood.

A layer of water surrounding the earth would filter harmful cosmic radiation that penetrates the earth's atmosphere. *(Figure 23.)* Long wave radiation would be able to pass through the canopy layer but short wave radiation like ultraviolet light would not. The canopy of water would have functioned the same way the ozone layer protects the earth today from short wave radiation. Water is often used to act as a successful shield to protect living things from the ill effects of radioactive material in atomic research plants.

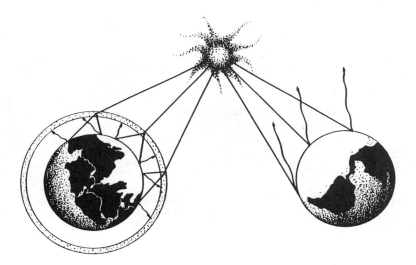

*Figure 22:*
*A canopied earth would have produced a stable climate from pole to pole as a result of the equal heating of the earth's surface. The absence of a canopy allows for unequal heating of the earth's surface, causing extreme climatic differences.*

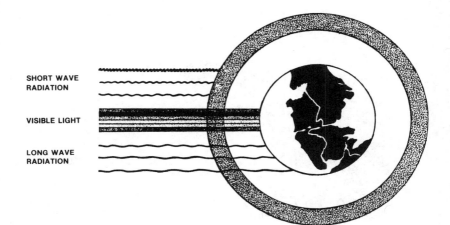

**SHORT WAVE RADIATION**

**VISIBLE LIGHT**

**LONG WAVE RADIATION**

*Figure 23:*
*A watery layer around the earth in the past would not allow*
*the passage of harmful short wave radiation to reach the earth.*

Short wave radiation is extremely harmful to life. As well as causing degenerative genetic changes to take place within the chromosomes of cells, short wave radiation is responsible for accelerating the aging process. Under the protection of a canopied earth we should find that plants and animals could grow much larger, be healthier and more vigorous, and live longer.

## Evidence for a Canopied Earth

As with any other model or theory, the authenticity or the degree of acceptance can only be measured by testing it against the observable evidence. We have looked at some of the major environmental conditions created by a layer of water surrounding the earth. Now we will look at some of the evidence that lends credibility to the model of the canopied earth.

## Subtropical Life from Pole to Pole

The canopy model suggests subtropical life would have lived from pole to pole as a result of uniform temperate conditions all over the world. Is there any evidence to indicate life lived under these kind of conditions in the past? Examining the fossil record gives us numerous examples of organisms which have lived in the past. It soon becomes obvious that climatic conditions must have been very different in the past than they are today.

For example, fossils of palm tree leaves have been found on the northern tip of Vancouver Island, Canada. *(Figure 24.)* These leaves are found encased in volcanic rock, indicating they were destroyed as a result of being quickly covered over by a volcanic eruption. This type of subtropical vegetation does not grow in this area today. Obviously, the climate must have been very different in this area in the past.

*Figure 24:*
*This fossilized imprint of a portion of a palm tree leaf was*
*found near Port Hardy, British Columbia, Canada. The leaf*
*has been encased by a flow of molten volcanic rock.*

Another area we could look at is the New Siberian Islands, situated north of Russia and within the Arctic Circle. *(Figure 25.)* Scattered throughout these islands are found the remains of tropical forests, gigantic fruit trees with green leaves and fruit frozen in the ice, as well as the remains of mammoths and other mammals. Obviously, this kind of life does not exist in this part of the world today. These findings were reported in the book, *The Mysteries of the Frozen Mammoths* page 76, written by Charles H. Hapgood.

The Spitsbergen Islands, north of Norway and also within the Arctic Circle, is another area where subtropical life has been found preserved. Donald Patten, on page 110 of his book, *The Biblical Flood and the Ice Epoch,* mentions palm tree leaves ten to twelve feet in length have been found in a fossilized condition in this area, along with fossilized subtropical marine life of various kinds. *(Figure 26.)*

Numerous finds have been made in Alaska to indicate life was much different in that area in the past than it is today. *National Geographic,* March, 1972, has an interesting article about the Alaskan tundra. In this article, the reader is told about the remains of gigantic camels, lions, horses, mammoths, tigers, sloths, and bison found frozen in layers of ice and mud. *(Figure 27.)* These animals do not live in this part of the world today, yet the evidence reveals they did in the past.

In the extreme southern hemisphere, very near the South Pole, the fossilized remains of luxuriant forests with tree trunks over three feet in diameter have been found. This is reported on page 44 of the book, *Those Astounding Ice Ages* by Hooker. Trees do not grow in this area today. Once again, the observable evidence confirms the biblical model of a canopied earth. Subtropical vegetation and animal life in the past have lived from pole to pole.

## Large Plants and Animals

What about the suggestion that plant and animal life would

be much larger in the past? If a canopied earth existed in the past, there should be numerous examples of gigantic plants and animals occurring in the fossil record. Let's look at some of these examples.

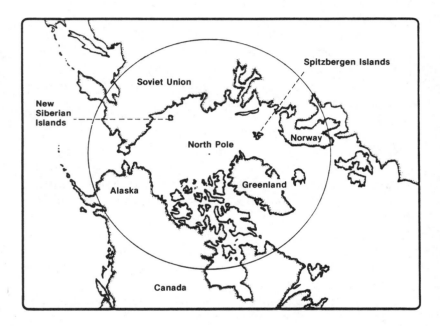

*Figure 25:*
*A prominent feature of the fossil record is the abundance of fossils within the polar regions that are characteristic of life living in a subtropical environment. Obviously, the climatic conditions in the polar regions must have been much different in the past than exist today.*

*Figure 26:*
*Fossilized remains of subtropical marine organisms have been found in the Spitsbergen Islands. These islands are located north of Norway and within the Arctic Circle.*

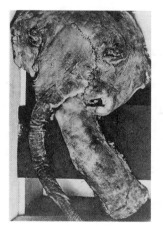

*Figure 27:*
*This frozen baby mammoth was dug out of the Arctic muck by Alaskan miners searching for gold. These great animals are often found with the last mouthful of food they were eating still in their mouths, indicating the freezing process must have occurred instantly.*

*The Green Kingdom,* a book published by Childcraft, illustrates a number of drawings of plants that lived in the past.
These drawings are based on information gathered from the
fossil record. *(Figure 28.)* On page 206, moss-like plants that
grew nearly three feet tall are shown. Today, moss plants grow
approximately two or three inches tall. On page 209, plants
that look like huge asparagus stalks are shown. They grew
over forty feet tall. The root systems of these plants are similar
to the hair-like root systems of onion plants like we see today. Obviously the roots of these plants did not have to go
deep into the soil in order to get moisture, nor anchor
themselves against winds and storms.

Horsetail reeds have been found in the fossil record that
grew over fifty feet tall. Today the horsetail reed grows in
marshy areas but only to a maximum height of four or five
feet. Fern-like plants grew in the past to heights of over fifty
feet high, compared to the bush-sized plants of today.

Insects have been found in the fossil record that are much
larger than their counterparts of today. For example,
cockroaches have been found over one foot in diameter;
dragonflies have been preserved with a wingspan of over three
feet. *(Figure 29.)*

Fossil remains of marine organisms are often much larger
than their counterparts of today. In the Sundance Canyon, near
Banff, Alberta, Canada, fossil clams have been found over
two feet in length. Nautiloid shells have been found in the
fossil record that are over nine feet in diameter. *(Figure 30.)*
Today, their existing descendants are only about eight inches
in size.

Giant animal fossils of many different kinds have been found
all over the world. *Giants From The Past,* a book published
by the National Geographic Society, shows many of these huge
creatures of the past no longer existing today. Fossil remains
of the hornless rhinoceros indicate it was over 17 feet tall;
*(Figure 31.)* pigs grew to be the size of cattle; camels were
over 12 feet tall; huge birds towered to a height of over 11 feet;

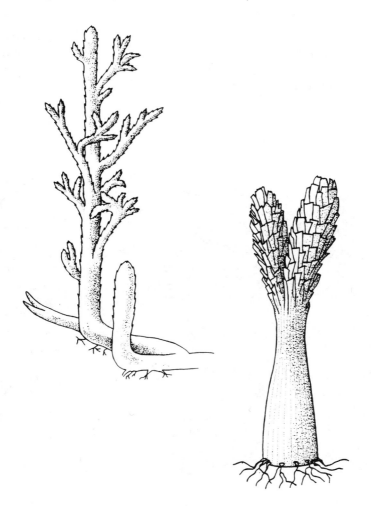

*Figure 28:*
*The fossil record shows that plants living in the past were very*
*different than plants living on earth today. Moss-like plants*
*grew over three feet in height compared to the few inches they*
*grow today. Plants that look like asparagus stalks grew over*
*forty feet in height, yet were supported by a very delicate root*
*system.*

giant beavers grew to be the size of a pig; deer antlers measured over 12 feet in width. Ground sloths that grow to the size of an average monkey today have been found in the fossil record over 18 feet in length. *(Figure 32.)*

*Figure 29:*
*The fossil record shows that dragonflies had wingspans as wide as three feet.*

One of the most prominent features of the fossil record is the abundance of huge reptile creatures. *(Figure 33.)* The most common reptile of the past is the dinosaur. Reptiles begin life by hatching from an egg, then growing larger and larger each year. The longer a reptile lives, the larger it gets. The dinosaur is one of the largest creatures that has ever lived on the face of this planet. In order for dinosaurs to have grown to the tremendous size as revealed by the fossil record, their life spans must have been much longer than reptile life spans of today. The protective canopy would certainly help to explain why the animals of the past grew larger and lived longer.

## The Life Span of Man

If the canopy model is correct, then there should be evidence to indicate the life span of man was much longer in the past. As we look at the scriptural account of the geneologies of men who lived upon the early earth, we see the average life span of original man was much longer than the average life span of man today.

If we look at a chart showing the life spans of men from Adam to Isaac, we would see a definite contrast between those who lived before and those who lived after the flood of Noah. *(Figure 34.)* In Genesis chapter five, the average age of man who lived before the flood was approximately 900 years. After the flood there is a marked deterioration of the long life spans. Within a 600-year period the longevity of life tapers from the 900-year average down to approximately 175 years in length.

The canopy model helps us understand why man lived so long before the flood. At the time of the great flood of Noah, the canopy collapsed upon the earth and provided one of the sources of the flood waters. The pre-flood earth canopy protected man from the harmful short wave radiation from the sun, which is known to accelerate the aging process. After the flood when the canopy was gone, the earth would have been exposed to short wave radiation and life spans would drop off sharply. As time went on, the short wave radiation would continue to cause degeneration to the genetic blueprints of life and be passed on to subsequent generations. The aging process would continue to accelerate. Today the average life span of man is approximately 70 to 80 years of age, nowhere close to the 900 years that men were living before the flood.

Once again, we see the Bible has given us keys for understanding past events. The scriptural insight into a pre-flood canopied earth helps us understand the longevity of early man as recorded in the Bible and answers many of the questions that result from observing the fossil record.

*Figure 30:*
*The fossilized remains of a nautiloid shell found in the foothills*
*of the Canadian Rockies reveals the gigantic size of these*
*creatures in the past. Nautiloid species living today are usually*
*only several inches in diameter.*

*Figure 31:*
*The hornless rhinoceros of the past grew to be over seventeen*
*feet tall. This creature is the largest land mammal that has*
*ever lived.*

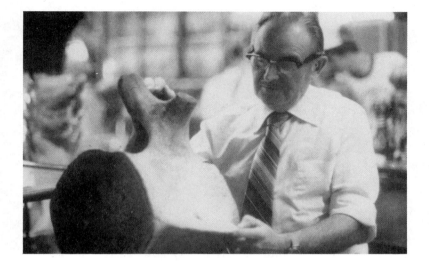

*Figure 32:*
*This huge vertebra, which is on display at the Glen Rose, Texas Museum, is claimed to be from the backbone of a giant sloth of the past.*

*Figure 33:*
*Dinosaur fossils are found in numerous locations around the*
*world. These huge reptiles are representatives of one of the*
*largest forms of life that have ever lived upon the face of the*
*earth.*

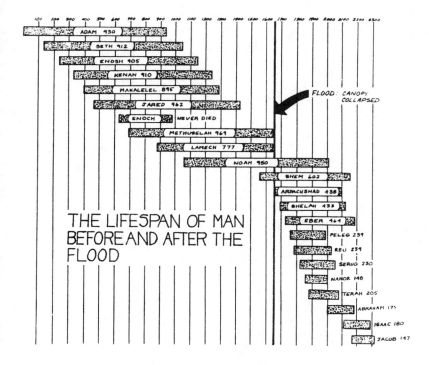

*Figure 34:*
*This chart depicts the biblical account of the age of men liv-*
*ing before and after the flood of Noah. It is apparent that the*
*life span decreases after the time of the flood. It would ap-*
*pear the extremely long life spans before the flood could be*
*attributed to the filtering of harmful radiation as a result of*
*the presence of a water canopy.*

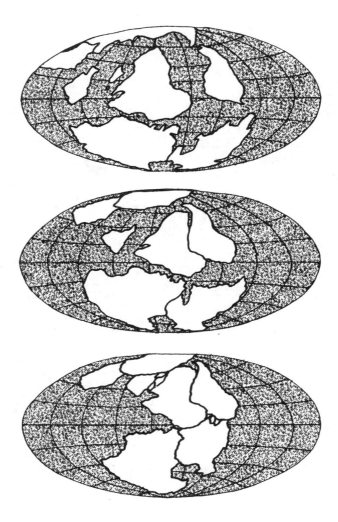

*Figure 35:*
*Conventional geological theory teaches that 200,000,000 years*
*ago land mass was together in one place. Over the proposed*
*millions of years of time, the one land mass broke apart and*
*gradually separated to the position the continents are found*
*today.*

# THE ONE LAND MASS

Another very important feature of the original earth the Bible tells us about is the land mass was all together in one location. Today when we look at a geographic map of the earth, it is apparent the land mass is divided into several continental bodies. Let's examine the Scriptures in order to find out more about what the original earth was like and look at the events which took place to bring about the division of the continents as we know them today.

The insight the Bible gives us regarding the formation of the original land mass is stated in Genesis 1:9-10:

> *And God said, Let the waters under heaven be gathered together unto one place, and let the dry land appear: and it was so. And God called the dry land Earth; and the gathering together of the waters called he Seas: and God saw that it was good.*

From these two verses of Scripture it is apparent the land mass was in one place at the time of creation.

## The Evidence from Geology

For generations individuals who have studied maps of the world have noticed the eastern and western hemispheres fit together like pieces of a jigsaw puzzle. In the early 1900s, some geologists proposed that the continents had been joined together at one time in the past history of the earth. They pointed out the coastlines of Africa and South America have similar geological layers containing identical fossils of plants and animals.

Geological discoveries made over the past several decades have confirmed the earth's land mass was originally all together in one place. This of course agrees with the account we are given in the Bible. However, the geological theory for the separation of the continents takes place over a time period of hundreds of millions of years. Keep in mind that the foundational principle of modern geology is based on the assumption the earth is billions of years old.

The most popular theory proposed by geologists for the origin of the continents is the theory of continental drift. This concept, often called global plate tectonics, has challenged the traditional evolutionary concept of a stable planet. Such a theory in the past would have been totally rejected, yet today it is widely accepted as a geological truth. The concept of plate tectonics advances the following view of the earth's history:

1. The earth's crust consists of several plates or sections. These plates could be compared to a cracked shell of a hard boiled egg. The plates float on the hot molten mantle which is beneath them. The earth's land surface and the ocean bodies rest upon these sections of the earth's crust.

2. Some 200 million years ago the earth's land mass was joined in one location. *(Figure 35.)* This super-continent has been often called Pangaea. For some reason the one large land mass began to split up and gradually separate.

3. Over millions of years of time the seven continents and the numerous major islands we observe today were gradually moved into their present positions.

The question of how and why the continents divided over 200 hundred million years ago is often discussed. *Science News* April 7, 1976, reported that a sudden event broke the continents apart. Recent theories have proposed that an object of cosmic origin may have slammed into the earth, causing the initial separation.

## The Biblical Account of the Division of the Earth

The biblical account of the division of the earth differs from the geological theory of division by the important factor of time. According to the Bible, the earth was divided in the days of a man named Peleg, who lived shortly after the period of time when the Tower of Babel was constructed. Genesis 10:25 states: "And unto Eber were born two sons: the name of one was Peleg; for in his days was the earth divided."

The Tower of Babel incident is described in detail in the Bible. *(Figure 36.)* At this time, man was beginning to repopulate the earth following the global flood of Noah. Genesis 11 describes the events which took place in the land of Shinar as man attempted to build a city and a tower to reach into the heavens. God had instructed man to scatter over the entire earth, but man chose to rebel against God. In order to bring an end to the construction of the Tower of Babel, God confounded their language and scattered them abroad. Following the scattering of the people over the surface of the earth, God divided the one land mass. This occurred during the days of Peleg.

The word *Peleg* in the Hebrew means a sudden division or a canalling by water. Certainly such a division of the earth's one land mass would bring about tremendous catastrophic events. The initial division of the land mass would not have separated the continents as far apart as they are today. As we shall see later, the biblical account for the history of the earth mentions numerous other global catastrophies which would have altered the earth's geography in recent historical times.

*Figure 36:*
*According to the biblical account of the history of the earth,*
*the division of the one land mass took place only a few thousand*
*years ago. This was at a period of time shortly following the*
*building of the Tower of Babel.*

# THE CREATION OF THE HEAVENLY BODIES

The biblical account of origins specifically mentions the creation of the heavenly bodies. Everyone at one time or another has looked up to the heavens and wondered how the heavenly bodies came into existence. *(Figure 37.)* According to the Bible the heavenly bodies were created on the fourth day of creation. Genesis 1:14-17 mentions the creation of the heavenly bodies and the purpose for which they were made:

> *And God said, Let there be lights in the firmament of the heaven to divide the day from the night; and let them be for signs and for seasons, and for days, and years: and let them be for lights in the firmament of the heaven to give light upon the earth: and it was so. And God made two great lights; the greater light to rule the day, and the lesser light to rule the night: he made the stars also. And God set them in the firmament of the heaven to give light upon the earth.*

One of the main purposes for the sun, moon, and the stars was the production of light for the earth. When God created these heavenly bodies, He created them with the light spanning the distance from the heavenly body to the earth.

According to the Bible, God created things in maturity. Adam was created as a mature man and not as a little baby. Trees were created as mature trees and not as little seedlings. When God created the heavenly bodies for the purpose of giving light to the earth, that purpose was fulfilled from the moment they were created.

A common question creationists are often asked deals with the long distances light must travel to the earth from the far away stars. If the creationist believes the earth is approximately 6000 years old, how do you explain the existence of light we see coming to the earth from stars millions of light years away? As previously mentioned, the purpose of these heavenly bodies was to give light to the earth. From the very moment the heavenly bodies were created, light immediately spanned the distance from the heavenly body to the earth.

*Figure 37:*
*According to the Bible, the heavenly bodies were created during the fourth day of creation. One of their main purposes was to give light to the earth.*

# THE CREATION OF LIFE

Another very important premise of the creation model is the creation of life. Genesis chapter one mentions God brought living things into existence on the third, fifth, and sixth days of the creation week. Although the Scriptures do not give a detailed description of every kind of plant and animal created, we are told that all living things on the earth appeared by the creative hand of God.

All life would have come on the scene suddenly, mature and fully developed. There would have been many more kinds of life present at the time of creation than what now exists on our planet. The greenhouse-like environment that was produced by the canopied earth would have provided optimal conditions for all kinds of life. Many forms of life would grow larger and be more vigorous. When we examine the evidence from the fossil record that is exactly what we find. There were many more kinds of life preserved in the fossil record than life that exists today. All kinds of life appear in a sudden profusion of complex, perfected forms with no simpler ancestral forms preceeding them. To any honest open-minded observer, the vast fossil evidence from all over the world confirms the Bible record of creation.

## After Its Kind

One of the most important features the Scriptures mention regarding the creation of life is the principle that life was designed with the built in mechanism of reproducing "after its kind." In each verse of Genesis chapter one that God mentions the creation of life, God specifically mentions the created form of life would "bring forth" or reproduce after its own kind.

The Scriptures clearly indicate life was created according to kinds. The kinds of life were outlined by specific genetic boundaries. The blueprints of life originally formed by the plan and design of the Creator provided limits for variation as the perpetuation of life took place from one generation to the next. For example, a dog would always reproduce by having puppies; cats would have kittens and so on. Never could one kind of life change and become something else. A dog would never have offspring that could suddenly develop wings and begin to fly.

According to this model, there would be a wide variation within a kind. *(Figure 38.)* The instructions for the coding of life contained within the chromosomes can provide multiplied forms of variation within certain limits. We know the human kind is made up of a variety of characteristics. There are many different features producing a wide variation in physical appearance, yet all these variances still belong within the human kind.

The dog kind is made up of many different sizes and shapes. It has been illustrated through the process of selective breeding that over 200 different varieties of dogs could be produced from one set of parents. The observable evidence indicates life can vary tremendously within a kind, but one kind can not change and become another. The theory of evolution is based on the premise that life develops and changes from simple forms to complex forms over long periods of time.

Another principle regarding the creation of life is that living things would have been coded with instinctive abilities and qualities from the very beginning. In other words, from the moment life came on the scene it was programmed with the necessary information required to perform various functions essential for life. Take for example a particular kind of animal behavior such as building a nest. A mother robin never has to teach its offspring the technique of building the kind of nest suitable for robins. The next generation always knows instinctively how to build a robin's nest. The robin doesn't dig a badger hole or construct a swallow's nest; the robin always builds a robin's nest. The biblical model suggests the knowledge and the ability to carry out many of life's requirements were in operation from the beginning. These were not things which had to be learned over long periods of time by trial and error.

*Figure 38:*
*The biblical model of creation teaches that life was created according to "kinds," and that each kind would reproduce within specific genetic boundaries. A kind would be capable of exhibiting a wide variation of characteristics but could never change and develop into another kind.*

# THE CREATION OF MAN

The creation of man took place on the sixth day of the creation week. Man was the focal point of the entire creation. Genesis 1:26-27 states:

> *And God said, Let us make man in our image, after our likeness: and let them have dominion over the fish of the sea, and over the fowl of the air, and over the cattle, and over all the earth, and over every creeping thing that creepeth upon the earth. So God created man in his own image, in the image of God created he him; male and female created he them.*

The Bible tells us man was created in the image of God. That does not necessarily mean that man had the same appearance as God, as we would understand physical features such as eyes, ears, and other bodily characteristics. It means man was created with abilities, attributes, and capacities like God. Man could think, feel, understand, and appreciate like God. As a result of being designed with these kinds of characteristics, man was a God-like being.

Original man was coded with wisdom, knowledge, and understanding from the very beginning. Adam and Eve, the first man and woman, would have been the most intelligent human beings who ever existed. Original man was designed to use one hundred per cent of his brain, not just the fraction of the brain's capacity that is used today by modern man. Adam and Eve did not start out as primitive brute-like beings. They were coded with complete knowledge, wisdom, and appreciation for the things of creation from the very beginning.

The most important aspect of the creation of man is that God made man as an intelligent being with a free will. Man was free to choose whether or not he would love, obey, and fellowship with his Creator. Man was not designed as a robot to be forced into a love relationship with God. A love relationship can only be established when there is a choice made by a willful decision of the two partners involved.

The Bible further tells us what took place as a result of the free choice that God gave man. We are given the account in Genesis of the fall of man, when Adam and Eve willfully chose to disobey God and surrender their will to Satan. Sin entered the world and from that point on was passed down from generation to generation. At the time of the fall, the whole creation fell with man and has continued to degenerate through the subsequent generations. The direction of the universe began to proceed in a direction from order to disorder. As a result of the sinful nature of man that began at the fall, the human race has been involved in terrible wickedness, corruption, and perversion. God has repeatedly brought about catastrophic judgments upon the earth to judge man for his wickedness and sin.

The first major judgment the Bible mentions is the great flood of Noah. In order for us to better understand what happened to the original perfect creation, it is necessary for us to examine what the Bible says took place during this event.

# THE DESTRUCTION OF THE ORIGINAL CREATION

After the fall of man, the perfect creation God had planned began to degenerate. As a result of the terrible wickedness and corruption which took place on the earth, God had no choice but to send judgment and bring destruction upon the original earth. The creation premise for the earth's origin and history is not complete unless we take into account the numerous catastrophic judgments of God upon sinful man.

*Figure 39:*
*The flood of Noah was a global event which brought judgment and destruction upon the original creation.*

The first major catastrophe affecting the earth was the flood of Noah. *(Figure 39.)* This global event completely devastated the original creation. There was a sudden destruction of plants and animals. Many kinds of life were completely destroyed. There was a sudden destruction of the most highly advanced civilization that has ever lived. The lush, global, subtropical environment that had existed over the entire planet was destroyed. There was a sudden rearrangement of the earth's geological features which took place on a global scale. Without question the great flood of Noah did more to change the features of the planet earth than any other event in history.

## The Events of the Flood

Genesis chapters seven and eight identify the major events which took place during the flood. Looking at an overview of these events will give us a better understanding of what happened to the original earth. The Scriptures mention that at the time of the flood the following events occurred:

1. The windows of heaven were opened.
2. The fountains of the great deep broke up.
3. Rain occurred for forty days and forty nights.
4. Tidal wave activity occurred on a global basis.
5. The crust of the earth rose and sank.

The Bible indicates God's wrath was poured out as "the windows of heaven were opened" (Genesis 7:11). Throughout Scripture when reference is made to "the windows of heaven" and the context regards judgment, it refers to material falling upon the earth from cosmic origin. *(Figure 40.)* God, using His own laws of nature, brought divine judgment upon the earth. He also brought about disturbances in the heavens affecting the stability of our earth. As the result of the close passage of other heavenly bodies near the earth, there have been tremendous gravitational and electromagnetic effects.

The flood description mentions one of the major occurrences was the fracturing of the earth's crust as "the fountains of the great deep [broke] up.'' *(Figure 41.)* This would trigger off volcanic eruptions on a global scale. Extreme amounts of volcanic ash, lava, super-heated water, and carbon dioxide would be poured out all over the land mass and the ocean beds. Marine organisms would be rapidly caught and destroyed by volcanic and sedimentary deposits. On the land, plant and animal life would be caught, destroyed, and covered over by thousands of feet of flood-deposited layers. All manner of life would be mixed and scrambled together and quickly buried.

Associated with the flood events would be hot cosmic debris falling from the heavens. This kind of activity happened at other periods of history when God poured out ''fire and brimstone'' upon the earth. The prophet Isaiah described the same kind of cosmic judgment being rained down when ''the windows from on high are open'' (Isaiah 24:18). At the time of the flood, hot meteoric iron, cosmic hydrocarbon gasses, flaming tar, and bitumin would have been rained down upon the earth.

The canopy of water which surrounded the original earth would collapse during all of this activity. This would create a large portion of the flood waters covering the earth. Torrential rain would occur in most areas of the earth; thousands of feet of ice and snow would be deposited in the polar regions. Great depths of cosmic ice would also be quickly deposited around the magnetic poles of the earth. Polar ice caps would form suddenly, catching subtropical plant and animal life in a moment of time.

The earth's crust was greatly disturbed at this time, as land masses rose and sank. *(Figure 42.)* Mountains were buckled up and valleys sank. (See Psalm 104:8, The Living Bible.) Entire civilizations were swallowed up into the earth. (See Ezekiel 26:19-20.) Areas that were once ocean beds became deserts.

Tidal activity took place on a global basis over several months. (See Genesis 8:1,3,5.) Waves would be ripping back and forth across the surface of the globe, carrying vegetation and animal material. All kinds of living material would be scrambled together, mixed with volcanic ash, volcanic mud, and other debris. Tidal waves bearing dead plants and animals from land and sea would be laid down in horizontal flood-deposited layers. Thousands of feet of deposition would occur in a very short period of time. Layer upon layer would form, as land masses rose and sank. *(Figure 43.)* Vegetation and animal life would be scrambled together, torn, and buried in the layers of the earth in no particular order. *(Figure 44.)*

This global flood took place in a time period of less than a year. As a result of this great catastrophe the original climate and environment were totally changed. Many varieties of plants and animals became extinct. Plant and animal life was buried in thousands of feet of volcanic deposits and sedimentary layers and quickly fossilized. Geological features over the entire face of the earth were altered.

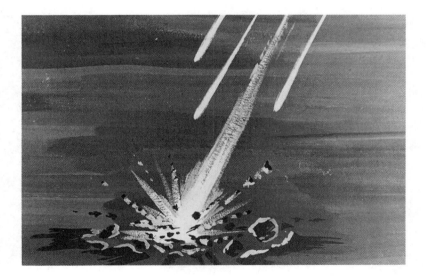

*Figure 40:*
*The phrase, "the windows of heaven were opened" refers to fire and brimstone material falling from the heavens.*

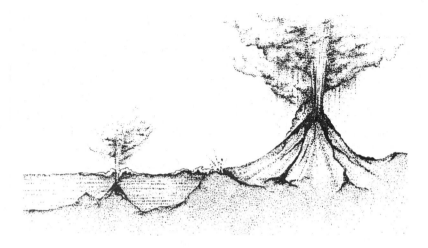

*Figure 41:*
*One of the major events at the time of the flood occurred when*
*the "fountains of the great deep [were] broken up" (Genesis*
*7:11). The earth's crust fractured both on land and under the*
*sea, creating volcanic activity on a global basis.*

*Figure 42:*
*The rising and sinking of land mass at the time of the flood*
*rearranged the earth's geological features.*

*Figure 43:*
*Evolutionary geological theory suggests the earth's layers were formed as the result of millions of years of gradual deposition. The biblical model claims the numerous layers of the earth are the product of catastrophic deposition of material over a short period of time.*

## Other Catastrophic Events

The great flood of Noah is only the first of a number of catastrophic judgments God brought upon the earth in recent historical times. *(Figure 45.)* The division of the continents took place shortly after the period of time when the Tower of Babel was constructed. Following this was the fiery destruction of Sodom and Gomorrah. In the time period around 1500 B.C., there were global catastrophies associated with the Exodus and Joshua's long day.

Other catastrophic events took place in the 700-800 B.C. period, as recorded in the books of Joel, Amos, and Isaiah.

At each of these time periods man reached high peaks of satanic influence and wickedness which God had to judge. All of these catastrophies had a part in further alterations to our planet and must be considered as we study the biblical account of the origin and history of the earth.

*Figure 44:*
*According to the biblical model of the flood, all kinds of life would have been caught and destroyed in the layers of the earth. Fossils should not be found in a sequential order of simple to complex.*

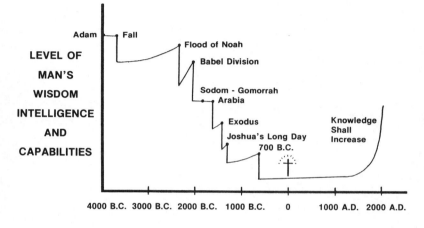

*Figure 45:*
*The above chart, representing approximately six thousand*
*years of recorded time, illustrates the biblical record of the*
*history of man. God used numerous catastrophic events to*
*bring about judgment on high peaks of civilization which have*
*been involved in wicked satanic practices.*

# THE EVOLUTION
# MODEL

# THE HISTORY OF EVOLUTION

The foundation of evolution is based upon the belief that the origin of all ordered complex systems including living creatures can be explained by the operation of natural laws without the initiation or the intervention of God. According to this line of thought, all living creatures including man are the product of billions of years of random chance events which have worked together to produce design and order out of randomness.

One hundred and fifty years ago such a theory for the origin and history of the earth and life would have been termed absurd. Today, however, those who reject the idea of random evolutionary processes being responsible for designing life and shaping the geological features of the earth are termed religious, unscientific fanatics.

Today, throughout the industrialized world, the moment children are able to respond to their environment, they are constantly bombarded with the doctrine of evolution. Childlike faith in the biblical concept of creation by the hand of God is ridiculed and rejected by the secular system of education. Humanistic thinking widely accepts evolution as a fact. It is commonly accepted that all living things are the product of evolution that has occurred in the past, that evolution is taking place today, and that evolution will continue to shape the destiny of life in the future.

## James Hutton

In order to better understand how the theory of evolution became so entrenched in the beliefs of our present generation, it is necessary to investigate how the theory was first initiated by some of the founding fathers. James Hutton (1726-1797) suggested the earth's geological layers were not the product of a global flood as had been believed up until that time, as taught by the Bible. The textbook *Biology,* written by Helena Curtis, makes the following statement:

> *It was geologists, more than biologists, who paved the way for evolutionary theory. One of the most influential of these was James Hutton (1726-1797). Hutton proposed that the earth had been molded not by sudden, violent events, but by slow and gradual processes—the same processes that can be seen in the world today.*
>
> *This theory of Hutton's that was known as uniformitarianism was important for three reasons. First, it implies that the earth has a living history and a long one. This was a new idea. Christian theologians, by counting the successive generations since Adam (as recorded in the Bible), had calculated the maximum age of the earth at about 6000 years. No one, as far as we know, had ever thought in terms of a longer period. Six thousand years is not enough time for such major evolutionary changes as the formation of new species to have taken place.*

This interesting background to the theory of evolution illustrates a very important point. Prior to the proposal of the evolutionary theory, the creation account for the origin and history of the earth was an acceptable model adequately explaining the observable evidence. The biblical account was then purposely rejected in favor of the evolutionary theory.

## Charles Lyell

Charles Lyell (1797 -1875), a British scientist, has often been called the founder of modern geology. Between 1830 and 1833, he published the three volumes of his *Principles of Geology,* which organized existing information about science. Lyell showed in his book that the earth had changed slowly and gradually through millions of years of time by the same processes going on today.

The motive behind Lyell's theory was not just the presentation of a new theory to explain the origin and history of the earth from a purely scientific point of view. The purpose of the evolution theory, as stated by several of its founders, was to show an alternate explanation for the origin of life could be made without giving the credit to a Creator. Francis Hitching, in his book called *The World Atlas Of Mysteries,* makes the following statement about Lyell and the reason behind the origin of evolutionary theory:

> *It was as much for political reasons as scientific reasons that the new theory of uniformitarianism grew up to challenge the biblical theory of creation. If the Bible told the truth, there was no way of peaceably challenging the monarchy in Britain, for sovereignty was supposed to descend from God to the King; but if the Bible could be shown to be inaccurate, particularly in respect to the key event of the Deluge, then the whole philosophical foundation on which the monarchy based its power would be shattered.*
>
> *That at any rate was the reasoning of a group of Whig lawyers and MP's, one of whom, Charles Lyell, published in 1830 his "Principles of Geology." In its 100 page introduction he argued brilliantly that the story of the Deluge was mythological and that the natural forces of erosion and the effects of volcanic uplift, taking place over millions of years of time, could easily explain the geological features of the earth.*

## Charles Darwin

Charles Darwin (1809 -1882) was a British naturalist who became famous for his theories on evolution. *(Figure 46.)* Like several other scientists before him, Darwin believed that through millions of years of time all species of plants and animals had evolved from a few common ancestors. Darwin acknowledged a debt to Lyell for providing the necessary time scale so the process of natural selection could operate. When Darwin's theory triumphed, the acceptance of uniformitarianism was assured.

Darwin was the grandson of the noted physician and naturalist Erasmus Darwin, who had proposed a theory of evolution in the 1790s. As a boy Charles Darwin often heard his grandfather's theories being discussed. Darwin studied medicine at the University of Edinburgh and theology at Cambridge University and received his degree there in 1831. His religious views, however, followed the common Victorian route from fundamental Christianity to agnosticism, and by the late 1830s he had abandoned his original Christian beliefs. This transformation was not entirely due to an accumulation of scientific evidence. Instead, Darwin complained of such things as the dubious history of the Bible, unacceptable actions of the Old Testament God, and the unbelievable doctrines of Christianity.

At the time of the publication of the *The Origin of Species* in 1859, Darwin considered himself a theist, basing his view on his internal conviction that the design he observed in the universe could not be the result of pure chance. As his life progressed, his views on evolution undermined his theism, leaving agnosticism in its place. He altered his original belief and accepted that the appearance of design in living things was actually the result of undesigned random chance. He reasoned that the evolutionary processes could not be the product of a loving, intelligent God because evolution involved the intense suffering of so many. He attributed the reality of man to the concept of natural selection rather than to the design of God which he had believed at one time.

*Figure 46:*
*Charles Darwin (1809-1882) is commonly remembered as one*
*of the founding fathers of the theory of evolution.*

## Evolution and the Church

Darwin's theory of evolution, based upon the idea of natural selection, set off a bitter controversy among scientists, religious leaders, and the general public. Noted British scientists such as Thomas Huxley and Alfred Wallace supported Darwin's work, and many different groups eventually accepted the theory of evolution.

Darwin's ideas had a tremendous impact on religious thought. Several British theologians soon suggested that the geological and biological information proposed by the new ideas from science clearly demonstrated the scientific inaccuracy of Genesis. Geology showed, they thought, that Genesis was not God's absolute word of truth for all times and all places.

After Darwin's idea of the origin and development of life became well known, others used the concept of evolution for developing theories about society. A number of new philosophies began to emerge based on the Darwinian theory. These ideas burst upon the world scene and carried implications which made a view of agnosticism and atheism respectable. For example, the German philosopher and social scientist Karl Marx (who is often called the founding father of the Communist movement) compared the struggle for survival among organisms to the struggle for power among social classes. Marx was so taken by the way Darwin was able to explain away the need for God regarding the origin of life that he endeavored to dedicate a book to Darwin which was against capitalism called *Das Capital*.

Marx and other humanists of his day believed the individual, not God, is the highest being. This view believes people make themselves what they are by their own effort, intelligence, and creative ability. The humanist view rejects the biblical premise that man has a fallen sinful nature which needs to be redeemed and believes man is headed along the evolutionary path to a higher consciousness. Thus we see evolution is the foundational premise of the humanistic view that man is becoming more and more a god-like being with the progression of time.

## Evolution and Education

The acceptance of the evolutionary doctrine soon spread throughout the academic world in spite of the opposition put forward by scientists and religious leaders. Most scholars who had swallowed the humanistic philosophy were proud of the fact they could explain the physical world around them without relying upon God. Evolution of life over millions of years of time coupled together with the concept of uniformitarianism soon became firmly entrenched throughout all the sciences. Today the theory of evolution is generally considered to be the most important fundamental concept of the biological sciences.

In many parts of the industrialized world, much of the controversy over evolution centered on the issue whether the theory should be taught in schools. Many people would not accept the theory of evolution because it conflicted with their belief that God is the Creator and sustainer of life. The Bible also states human beings were created in the image of God, and thus were elevated above all other forms of life. Because of this view by the majority of people, the teaching of evolution in the public schools in the United States occurred through a gradual process over many years.

The first major confrontation regarding the teaching of evolution in public schools occurred at the famous Scopes trial which took place in Tennessee in 1925. The effect of the trial on education was felt for many years, as most schools avoided teaching evolution and publishers produced texts that hardly covered the topic. For years following the Scopes trial the creation-evolution controversy was not a high-priority issue. The issue lay dormant until the 1950s, when there was a growing concern amongst educators that science teaching in the public schools needed to be upgraded with evolutionary teaching.

In the 1960s, a group of biologists received a grant from

the National Science Foundation to revamp the high school biology curriculum. These biologists, called the Biological Sciences Curriculum Study group, (B.S.C.S.) produced a series of biological textbooks that used evolution as the major unifying theme. The books the B.S.C.S. produced were widely adopted, and by the 1970s over half the students taking high school biology in North America were studying biology using these materials.

The reappearance of evolution in high school textbooks brought a strong reaction once again from people who believed in the biblical view of creationism. Strong resistance was expressed before school boards and government legislators, indicating evolution should be banned from the classroom. Many argued the teaching of evolution in the schools in the United States was against the law. However, when the issue was brought before the U.S. Supreme Court in 1968, the court ruled the banning of teaching of evolution was unconstitutional because it favored a particular religious viewpoint over others. After this ruling, creationists attempted to show that the biblical model for origins is a credible alternative to the theory of evolution, and that both views should be presented side by side in the classroom for the student to evaluate.

Resistance to this approach for the study of origins and to the re-evaluation of evolution has been strong. As creationists continued to make their view regarding the origin and history of life known, the creation-evolution controversy became widespread. Most evolutionists argued that scientific creationism is not science. They believe the motive behind the movement is a narrow fundamentalist interpretation of Christianity and that the disciples of creationism are attempting to infiltrate science with their religious views. Educators who are firm believers in the evolutionary doctrine see the admission of scientific creationism in the public school classroom as a wholesale destruction of the theory of evolution.

And thus we see a brief history behind the well established view of evolution. The pattern revealed by the study of the history of the evolution-creation controversy holds true with what the apostle Paul wrote in Romans 1:19-20, 25:

*Because that which may be known of God is manifest in them; for God hath showed it unto them. For the invisible things of him from the creation of the world are clearly seen, being understood by the things that are made, even his eternal power and Godhead; so that they are without excuse: because that, when they knew God, they glorified him not as God, neither were thankful; but became vain in their imaginations, and their foolish heart was darkened. Professing themselves to be wise, they became fools . . . who changed the truth of God into a lie, and worshiped and served the creature more than the Creator, who is blessed for ever.*

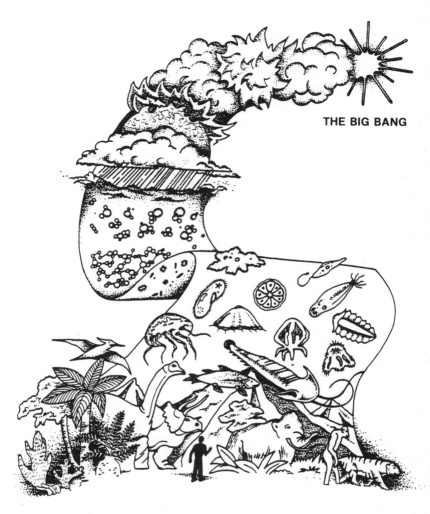

THE BIG BANG

*Figure 47:*
*The above chart represents a typical textbook drawing il-*
*lustrating a basic evolutionary premise—the Big Bang.*
*Evolutionists believe all the order and complexity observed*
*in the entire universe can be traced back to an initial explo-*
*sion that took place billions of years ago in the past.*

# THE BIG BANG

Everyone recognizes the universe had to have a beginning. Yet, it is difficult for the human mind to comprehend what might have taken place when the universe began. Was the creative force something that can be described by the laws of physics, or did it come into existence by the creative power of an almighty God? The most common explanation proposed by evolutionists is that at the beginning of time there was a tremendous explosion they have called the *big bang*.

According to this theory, all design and complexity that can be observed in the universe can be traced back to this initial explosion. *(Figure 47.)* Scientists suggest this explosion took place somewhere between 9 and 18 billion years ago. At that time, scientists claim, all the matter in the universe was packed together in a dense mass at temperatures of many trillions of degrees.

Following this explosion, random chance processes taking place over enormous periods of time are supposedly responsible for the formation of order from disorder. Atoms and molecules supposedly came together to form heavenly bodies like our solar system; non living molecules came together to form simple life; simple life progressed over millions of years of time and random processes to form complex life.

The big bang theory for the origin of the universe is popularly accepted by many evolutionists as an actual fact. Articles are often written in various science journals which give the impression the big bang has been proven beyond doubt. For example, the following quotation from *Science Digest,* May 1981, page 36 states:

> *The first billion, billion, billion, billionth of a second—and then, using a simple system of logic, we can now deduce in exact detail what happened during the the first second of creation. Recently we have*

*learned that some of the most dramatic events in the life of the universe took place before it was one second old. To the astonishment of the lay person, scientists are pushing back the barriers of time to reconstruct the the first billion, billion, billion billionth of a second.*

## The Big Bang and the Observable Evidence

From a logical point of view, it is difficult to accept an explosion as the basis for all design and complexity in the universe, especially since all the explosions ever observed have always brought about chaotic disorder.

For example, one of the greatest explosions in North America took place when Mt. St. Helens erupted. That particular explosion brought about terrible destruction and chaotic disorder. Our common sense tells us no intelligent person would ever attempt to blow up an object with the hope of obtaining another object of greater complexity, no matter how much time was allowed. In other words, it is a plain simple fact: explosions produce disorder out of order.

## Second Law of Thermodynamics

The laws of physics also contradict the big bang hypothesis. Every system allowed to proceed on its own always goes in a direction from order to disorder. This law of the universe is more commonly know as the second law of thermodynamics.

A few examples of how this law works will help to illustrate the impossibility of an explosion ever bringing about order from disorder. *(Figure 48.)* If you were to take a number of bricks and stack them in a neat ordered pile, given time, the pile would eventually break down and become disordered. Or if you were to take a brand new car, place it in a garage and leave it there for one hundred years without using it, it would eventually deteriorate, not become something better. Or all of us can relate to the process of our bodies aging. Given time, the cells of our bodies begin to malfunction; we become older and eventually die. We are aware that the sun is burning out as it uses up hydrogen that is not being replaced. All processes left to proceed by themselves must always go in a direction from order to disorder.

Logic and the plain observable evidence contradict the suggestion that an explosion was the creative force behind the beginning of the universe. The only other logical explanation which seems reasonable is the foundational principle of the creation model: ''In the beginning, God . . .'' (Genesis 1:1).

## THE SECOND LAW OF THERMODYNAMICS

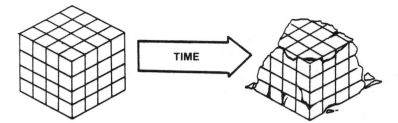

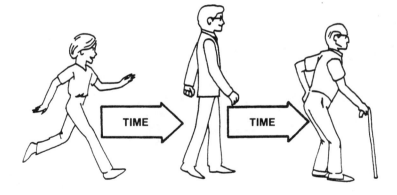

*Figure 48:*
*Given the factor of time, all systems left on their own proceed*
*in a direction from order to disorder.*

# THE ORIGIN OF LIFE FROM NON LIFE

A basic premise of the evolution model is that life is the product of random chance processes which have taken place over millions of years of time. A lot of speculation has been made regarding the formation of life from non-living particles. Many scientists have made the transition from non-life to life sound like a very natural and common process. The following statement is made by a scientist referring to this very subject:

> *We can make inspired guesses, but we don't know for certain what physical and chemical properties of the planet's crust, its ocean and its atmosphere made it so conducive to such a sudden appearance of life. We are not certain about the amount and the forms of energy that permeated the environment in the planet's early days. Thus the problem that scientists face is how to explain the suddenness with which life appeared on this young (4.6 billion year old) planet earth. This is a question that has plagued us ever since the nineteenth century, when scientists first began to accept the concept of biological evolution and to dismiss the possibility that life had been created in its present complexity by some supernatural agency. That raised the question of how this extraordinary phenomenon called life could possibly have come to be by accident.*

*Omni,* Isaac Asimov, November, 1983, page 58.

Asimov makes the statement that science has dismissed the possibility life could have been brought into existence by a supernatural creative being. In place of a Creator, he suggests the best alternative is nothing more than an "inspirational guess." Once again we see the process which takes place when man rejects the truth that has been planted in his heart and begins to imagine an alternative for God as the Creator.

## The Spontaneous Generation of Life

Several hundred years ago, it was commonly believed living things could be produced from non-living things by the process of spontaneous generation. People believed if garbage was left outdoors over a period of time, it would eventually turn into maggots, flies, and rats.

A man by the name of Francesco Redi decided he would prove to the world scientifically that living things can not be produced from non-living material. He placed some garbage outdoors and covered it with fine mesh so that flies and rats were unable to come in contact with the garbage. By doing this experiment, Redi proved to his generation that living things can not be produced from non-living material by the process of spontaneous generation.

The idea that people of the past actually believed in spontaneous generation seems unbelievable to us today. Scientists of the twentieth century would laugh at the simple experiment Redi used to convince the intellectuals of his day that they were wrong.

And yet, the theory of evolution stands on a premise very much like the idea of the spontaneous generation of life that was accepted as scientifically valid in the past. Evolution theory accepts without question that non-life can become life by a process taking place over millions of years of time guided by nothing more than random chance events.

## The Law of Biogenesis

But what does the observable evidence tell us? The observations made when we examine living things is that all life originates from life which already exists—life comes from pre-existing life. This is commonly known in the field of biology as the law of biogenesis.

The cell is described by biologists as the basic unit of life. No scientist has ever observed a cell originating from the raw materials that make up a cell by spontaneous processes. Controlled experimentation by the advanced technology of our day has never been able to produce a living cell. Cells can only come from cells that are already in existence.

Multicellular organisms never arise spontaneously from non-living material. The perpetuation of life can only take place as living things beget a new generation of living things. Plants produce seed which produce new plants of the same kind; cats produce kittens which develop into mature cats. Life can only originate from life which already exists. The powerful evidence that clearly supports the law of biogenesis indicates that the facts agree with the biblical premise of how life began.

# TIME

One of the most important principles of the evolution model is the concept of long periods of time. The entire theory of evolution is based on the presumption the earth is billions of years old. Over these supposed billions of years the origin and development of life has occurred. In order for this concept of evolution to seem the least bit possible, time is absolutely essential. Time becomes the magic factor. It makes the impossible seem probable.

What happens if long periods of time are not available for the evolution model? What would happen if the proposed billions of years of time for the earth's history were suddenly shrunk to only a few thousand years? Would it still be reasonable to suggest the evolutionary process was a possibility?

## The Importance of Time

Have you ever stopped to think how important time is to the concept of evolution? Long periods of time can make an idea that doesn't seem possible appear to be possible. The following illustration will help to clarify this point.

Suppose someone wanted to develop a new theory for the origin of man. This theory claimed that a single celled organism like an amoeba could change and develop into a human in only a few seconds of time. *(Figure 49.)* Obviously, this kind of a hypothesis would be termed absolutely ridiculous by the scientific community. It would be totally rejected as nothing more than a fairy tale or fantasy.

Now let's see what the factor of a long period of time does to this same proposition. Suppose someone suggested that a single celled oranism like an amoeba could develop into a human being over millions of years of time. Would this kind of hypothesis be acceptable by the scientific community? The answer to this question is yes. In fact, such a theory for the origin and development of the human kind is the very basis of the evolutionary theory.

Almost everyone has seen the typical Darwinian tree of life. *(Figure 50.)* Many textbooks on the subject of the origin and development of life show a chart which depicts the development of various kinds of life from the amoeba, progressing to man at the top of the tree. Long periods of time have made a ridiculous idea seem credible.

The evolutionary theory is built upon the premise that time is essential for simple forms of life to develop into complex forms of life. If you remove the proposed millions and billions of years of time that evolution suggests, the whole theory collapses.

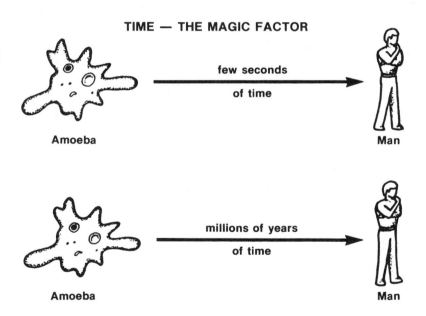

*Figure 49:*
*Extremely long periods of time make a ridulous explanation for the origin of man seem possible.*

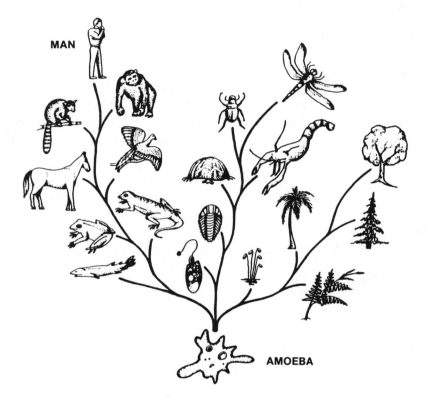

*Figure 50:*
*This Darwinian tree of life chart illustrates the evolutionary concept of the development of higher forms of life from lower forms of life over millions of years of time.*

# DESIGN—A PRODUCT OF CHANCE

Evolutionists believe the design observed in the universe and the design observed in living things are the product of chance. According to this theory, the sun and the planets making up the solar system are the end product of the condensation of a nebulous cloud of dust. The earth with all its essential qualities which permit the existence of life just happened by some chance process. Complex life occurred by random chance processes without a master planner or designer.

Biology is the field of science dealing with the study of living things. Biologists agree the more they study the complex structures and systems that make up living things, the more incredible becomes their view of the complexity of life. In an attempt for us to catch a glimpse of the complexity of living things, let's look at the basic unit of life—the cell.

## The Cell

All living organisms are made up of units called cells. For example, the human body is made up of over 100 trillion single cells. Some of these cells are so small that a million of them could occupy a space no larger than a pin head.

It would be fair to say that a single cell is the most complex structure known to man. It is even more complicated than a human being, because every human being originates from one. Every one of us began from a single cell formed as a result of the union of a sperm and egg cell from our parents that fused together at the time of fertilization. The blueprint for the construction of our entire make up was contained within the chromosomes in the nucleus of that first cell.

Over the past several decades a tremendous amount of research in cell biology has unfolded a whole new universe of complexity. *(Figure 51.)* With the use of high powered electron microscopes, biologists have broken through the cell's barrier of invisibility and have been able to take a close up view of what lies within the walls of the cell. They have found a magnitude of complexity staggering to the human mind.

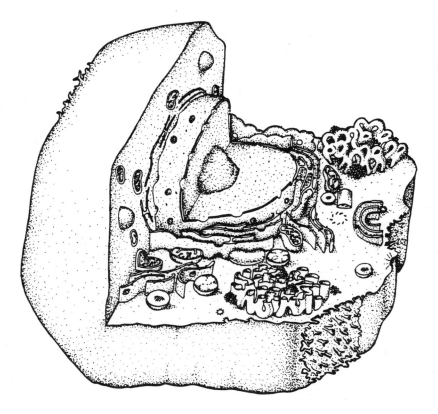

*Figure 51:*
*The cell is the basic unit of all living things. Observations of the components making up the cell reveal a degree of complexity unequaled by any other structure in the universe.*

The cell has turned out to be a micro-universe containing trillions of molecules. These molecules are the structural building blocks for countless complex structures performing chains of complex biochemical reactions with precision. One biologist has made the following statement regarding the complexity of a cell:

> *Even if we knew all there is to know how a cell works, we would still be baffled. How nerve cells create emotions, thoughts, behavior, memory and other perceptions cannot yet, if indeed ever, be described in the language of molecular biology.*

National Geographic, September, 1976, page 355.

Most of us have seen simplified diagramatic representations of cells depicting various cellular components and their function. A single cell surrounded by a cellular membrane exhibits the same degree of complexity as a city with all of its systems of operation, communication, and government. There are power plants that generate the cell's energy; factories that produce enzymes and hormones essential for life; complex transportation systems that guide specific chemicals from one location to another; membrane proteins that act as barricades controlling the import and export of materials across the cellular membrane. The following diagram and chart will help to illustrate some of these stuctures and their functions in more detail. *(Figure 52.)*

**membrane proteins**

> *These molecules span the exterior cell membrane and act as a monitor for informing the cell what is outside its boundaries.*

**endoplasmic reticulum**

> *A network of channels which stores and carries proteins from factory locations to other locations in the cell.*

**ribosomes**
> *Factory locations for the production of proteins.*

**lysosomes**
> *Structures that act as digestive organs, breaking down food into particles the cell can use for cellular processes.*

**golgi**
> *Structures that transport proteins, carrying them from the factory locations to the exterior membrane.*

**mitochondria**
> *These structures are the power plants of the cell, producing the fuel that gives the cell its energy.*

**cell membrane**
> *The exterior covering of the cell which regulates what enters and leaves the cell.*

**microtubules**
> *These long hollow tubes are the structures which give the cell its shape.*

**nucleus**
> *The nucleus contains the data center which governs all the cell's activities. It contains the chromosomes which make up the blueprint for future generations.*

We can see that every minute structure within a cell has a specific function. Without the full complement of all these structures, the cell can not function. In fact, even the slightest malfunction within the cell can bring about the immediate termination of its existence. How unbelievable it seems that such awesome complexity could have arisen by chance.

## DNA—The Blueprint of Life

DNA is the molecule of heredity. This molecule is responsible for the perpetuation of life as it is passed down from one generation to the next. *(Figure 53.)*

Every one of us started out from a tiny cell no larger than the period at the end of this sentence. The nucleus is the area within the cell that contains the DNA molecules which make up the blueprints of life. All of the coded information required for the development of our entire bodies originated from the DNA of that first cell. It can be said the DNA molecule functions like a computer, only with a far greater degree of complexity. Imagine the amazing design and order required to carry out the instructions for the development of the entire human body. Is it possible that this could have originated by chance?

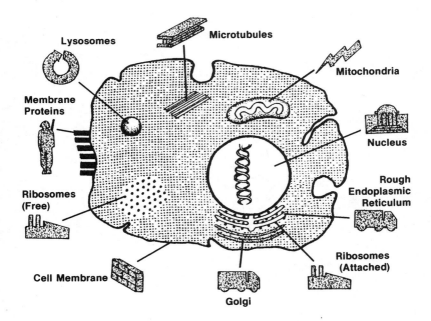

*Figure 52:*
*This simplified diagram illustrates some of the key structures found within a cell. Each structure has a specific function which contributes to the general well being of the cell.*

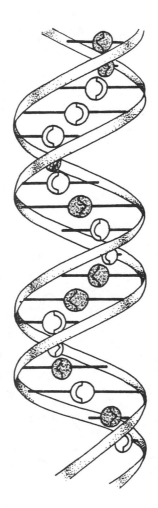

*Figure 53:*
*The DNA molecule is described as a double-stranded helical structure resembling a spiral staircase. The frame of the helix is formed of sugarphosphate units. The rungs are formed by the four nitrogenous bases adenine, guanine, thymine and cytosine. The specific order of these four bases determines the nature of the information coded by the DNA molecule.*

The DNA molecule is so minute and compact, it is hard for our human minds to comprehend. Perhaps the following illustration will help to give us a better understanding. The number of human beings living on the earth has been estimated to be somewhere between 4.5 and 5 billion people. If it were possible to reduce every individual to the original blueprint from which he originated, what size of a container would be required to store the blueprints for the entire world's population? Answer: a container the size of an aspirin tablet.

Once again, we are staggered when we consider the awesome complexity of life. It becomes absurd when we attempt to consider that evolution believes that the origin and complexity of life came about by random, accidental processes. Such a claim is a contradiction to sound, logical thinking.

## The Principle of Design

A common observation can be made as we examine objects around us in the physical realm. Any object which exhibits design must originate by a designer. This follows the well-accepted principle of cause and effect. In order for an effect to be observed there must be a cause. Never can the effect be greater than the cause. These principles are so commonly accepted that we never question their importance.

Let's look at some examples which will help to illustrate this principle. No one would ever suggest a beautiful painting originated by chance; the painting obviously required an intelligent artist who had an inspiration for a particular image and expressed it with the use of his artistic capabilities. Books do not come about by the spontaneous accumulation of sentences; they must be written by someone who has an idea, then expresses that idea in the form of written words. An object like a table does not come into existence by chance; it must be designed by someone with an idea for its structure and then it is constructed by a craftsman.

Any non-living object which exhibits design must have a designer. Design requires a designer. We have already mentioned that living things exhibit design far beyond the degree of complexity found in paintings, books, and tables. Is it reasonable to suggest that life could have arisen without a designer? When the observable evidence is examined, it becomes very apparent that what the Bible says about the origin of life by special creation and the purposeful design of an intelligent, eternal Creator must be true.

## Bionics

Some of the most amazing inventions man has ever made have come about by the careful study of mechanisms which are in operation in nature. The field of bionics is a specialized field of biological engineering that specifically attempts to mimic processes found in nature that could benefit mankind. The phrase *bionic comparison* refers to these inventions. Let's look at some examples of bionic comparisons.

An amazing system found in nature is the bat's sonar system. *(Figure 54.)* For years, men who studied bats tried to find out how these creatures could find their way in the dark. It was eventually discovered that the bat's ability to navigate was by the use of transmitting sound vibrations. The bat sends out high-pitched ultrasonic signals from its vocal organs that bounce off anything in its path. The bat then perceives the signal bounced back to it, and the bat's brain is able to make the necessary response in its flight pattern and to determine what the object is. This is a truly amazing system of design that scientists claim the process of evolution has developed over millions of years of time.

Man-made radar and sonar systems were designed by studying the bat's system. *(Figure 55.)* These highly advanced technological inventions transmit frequencies and measure the time required for these frequencies to be bounced back to the transmitting device. Radar has been heralded as a great accomplishment produced by the intelligence of mankind.

The human eye is another amazing system biologists have often compared to the operation of a video recording system. *(Figure 56.)* As you are reading this page, light is reflected from the page to your eyes. The light then passes through an opening in the eye called the pupil. The size of the opening, and thus the amount of light allowed to pass through the pupil, is controlled by muscles in the iris. The iris closes down in bright light and opens up when the light becomes dim. The light then passes through a lens. Eye muscles control the shape of the lens, focusing the image that you are viewing onto a light sensitive screenlike retina at the back of the eyeball. Cells in the retina convert the light energy into an electrical stimulus which is then transferred to the brain. The brain then records the information the eye has perceived and it is stored there for as long as you will live.

A video system engineered by the design of man functions in very much the same way as the eye. *(Figure 57.)* Light reflected by objects is controlled by a mechanical iris and focused by a lens within the video camera. The light energy is converted to an electrical signal, then transmitted to a video recorder where the information is stored for playback at a later time. No one would ever suggest that a video system is the product of random processes of chance over millions of years of time, yet the eye, which is far more complex, is commonly attributed to the process of evolution.

Another bionic comparison would be the human brain and a computer. The brain is the most complex computer ever studied. Scientists have calculated that over thirty billion cells called neurons make up its structure. Each neuron may connect with other neurons as much as sixty thousand times. Your brain has recorded every stimulus your sensory organs have perceived throughout your entire life. The brain monitors and controls thousands of activities taking place in your body without your awareness by first receiving signals, making an analysis, then sending out information for the appropriate response. There has never been a computer designed by man which would even begin to compare to the complexity of the human brain.

By looking at these examples of bionic comparisons, we can see a pattern of logic. There is no question in our minds that inventions made by man are the result of intelligent design and planning. There is a zero possibility that they could have arisen by spontaneous chance. Why is it not logical to accept that the living systems from which they have been copied are the product of design as well? The evidence is overwhelmingly in favor of the premise that life is the handiwork of a Creator.

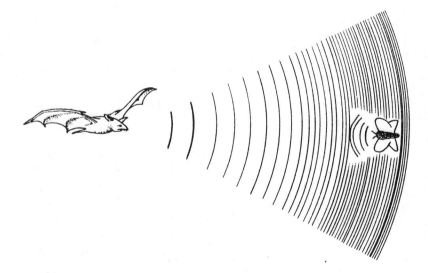

*Figure 54:*
*Sound waves emitted by the bat strike an object and echo back to its ears. On the basis of these echoes, bats can navigate skillfully through a dark room strung with wires or catch an insect as small as a fly.*

*Figure 55:*
*Advanced electronic radar equipment did not arise by chance.*
*It is the product of man's engineering and design capabilities.*

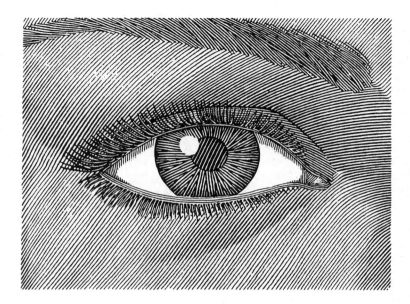

*Figure 56:*
*The theory of evolution teaches that complex organs like the*
*human eye were brought into existence without the direction*
*of an intelligent Creator.*

*Figure 57:*
*An electronic video system carries out similar functions that are accomplished by the human eye and brain. It would be ridiculous to suggest that a video camera and recorder came into existence by random chance events.*

# THE PROGRESSION OF LIFE

The evolutionist looks about the world of living organisms and sees that some are simple while others are very complex. He then arranges or classifies living things in an orderly sequence from simple to complex.

This idea of the development or progression towards a higher order of complexity over long periods of time is another fundamental principle of the evolution model. According to this theory, the development of new forms of life depends on the occurrence of mutations coupled together with a process called natural selection.

We have already examined the importance of time as one of the fundamental principles of evolution. But what about the idea that mutations and natural selection could bring about the production and development of new forms of life? Let us examine these two factors in more detail.

**Mutations**
**Simple life** ---------------------------- ❭ **Complex life**
**Natural Selection**

## Mutations

A mutation is a change in the genetic code. Mutations are often described as mistakes that occur in the DNA molecule which make up the blueprint of life. According to the evolutionary theory, mutations are partly responsible for bringing about an improvement in the quality of life.

We see that 99.99% of all mutations bring about harmful or lethal end products. How is it possible to suggest a .01%

chance could be the factor responsible for shaping new life forms? Former Nobel Prize winner Albert Szent Gyorgi had this to say about mutations:

> *To improve a living organism by random mutation is like saying you could improve a Swiss watch by dropping it and bending one of its wheels or axis. Improving life by random mutation has the probability of zero.*

Numerous experiments have been done by scientists in an attempt to show how mutations could bring about new varieties of life. For example, the fruit fly has been bombarded with every environmental variation that can be imagined in order to cause mutations to occur. *(Figure 58.)* Heat, pressure, chemicals, and radiation have effectively caused mutational changes to the fruit fly, but in the vast majority of cases these mutations are harmful or degenerative.

Often evolutionists argue that a series of mutations over long periods of time are required to bring about a major change to an organism. This certainly does not explain how complex organs like lungs, hearts, kidneys, and sexual reproductive organs could suddenly appear. Perfection of such organ systems is essential for the survival of organisms. It is obvious that creatures with such highly specialized structures essential for survival could not manage to exist while these structures and functions were evolving. Complex organ structures must be fully functional the first time they appear.

## Natural Selection

Natural selection has been defined as nature's way of selecting or choosing the best suited for a particular environment. The theory of evolution proposes that given time and the right trait combinations, organisms suited for their environment will survive and be successful. Darwin made this a very important part of the mechanism for his theory of evolution.

There is no question that natural selection does take place. The environment very obviously selects out the best suited for certain conditions. Scientists recognize that natural selection only preserves the best of what already exists for these environmental conditions, but it does not change one kind of life into another.

Let's look at an illustration to see how the process of natural selection actually works. Suppose you were to take a St. Bernard and a Chihuahua to the Arctic Circle and subject these animals to extremely cold temperatures. *(Figure 59.)* What would happen to these two different varieties of dogs, given the same environmental conditions? Obviously the Chihuahua would not be able to withstand the cold environment, yet the St. Bernard would be well suited to survive. In this example, the cold temperature has selected the St. Bernard. The environment acts as a selecting factor for choosing the best of what already exists, but it does not change one kind of life form into another.

## The Observable Evidence

The fossils provide us with an observable record of life that has lived on this planet in the past. If the claim that evolution makes about the progression of life from simple to complex over long periods of time is true, then there must be ample evidence to support this idea.

It is interesting to note there is no life that exists today superior to similar related varieties of the past. In fact, there are often many more varieties that lived in the past than what are presently alive today. These facts are an absolute contradiction of the foundational claims of evolution that many varieties of life evolved from inferior primitive forms to superior perfected forms. No such evidence is to be found in the fossil remains of life that has lived in the past.

The chambered nautilus, a type of marine shell organism, is an example which confirms the facts that we have just mentioned. In the past there were over 3500 varieties of these

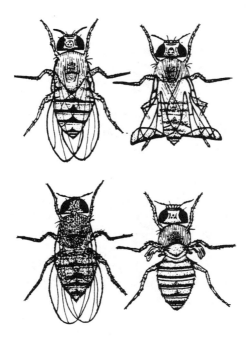

*Figure 58:*
*The fruit fly is commonly used in genetic experimentation. Numerous mutant strains have been observed including changes in eye color, wing size and shape, abdomen markings, and bristle arrangement. However, nothing other than a fruit fly has even been produced.*

*Figure 59:*
*The Chihuahua and the St. Bernard, both members of the dog kind, would respond differently to extremely cold climatic conditions.*

shells, some measuring over nine feet in diameter. Today there are only six varieties that have survived, and they are only about eight inches in diameter. The evidence indicates this particular organism has decreased dramatically in size and in numbers.

Often fossils that are alleged to be millions of years old show no difference at all from their living counterparts. A bat fossil that is shown on the front cover of *Science*, December 9,1982, is claimed to be 50 million years old, and yet it is identical to the bat of today. In *National Geographic,* January, 1981, page 134, a photograph is shown of a roach fossil alleged to be 300 hundred million years old. As the article states: "roaches have changed but little since their debut over 320 million years ago."

In *National Geographic*, September, 1977, page 423, there are several examples of insects preserved in amber. A mosquito supposed to be 40 million years old is identical to the mosquito of today. An ant that is supposed to be 100 million years old is identical to the ant of today. A praying mantis alleged to be 40 million years old is exactly like the praying mantis of today. This particular article concludes: "There is no evolution in the golden amber window of the past." It is obvious from the observable evidence shown from the fossil record, life has either remained the same, become extinct, or it has degenerated. There is no evidence to indicate life is in the process of developing and becoming more complex. Ecologists are telling us many life forms are headed towards extinction at a very rapid rate. This is exactly what we would expect, given the biblical model of the origin and history of life on this planet.

As observations are made of the numerous varieties of living things, it is certainly fair to ask how such variability has come about. In fact, those who reject the biblical account of Noah's Ark ridicule the idea that the present life forms we observe today could be traced back to ancestors that were preserved at that time.

Creationists do not deny there has been tremendous variation that has occurred in living things. In fact, the study of the laws of genetics has confirmed this creation premise over and over again. The creation model believes the number of possible varieties of a particular kind which can be produced depends on the number of combinations that can occur by the mixing of the genetic coding that already exists within a kind. Thus, it is possible for new combinations of genetic material that have always been in existence to produce new characteristics that have never been observed. However, the mixing of genetic material is limited by boundaries that are specified according to the created kinds that God originally brought into existence. One kind of life can not change and become another kind, as evolution claims.

Creationists also believe the environment plays an important role in selecting the best suited for certain conditions. Creationists recognize that the variation of genetic combinations, in conjunction with natural selection, is the mechanism which allows adaptation to occur and the perpetuation of life to take place.

*Figure 60:*
*A fundamental principle of the evolution model is the belief
life has progressed from simple to complex over millions of
years of time. If this supposition is true, there should be
numerous examples of life forms exhibiting the transition from
one kind to another.*

# ARE THERE MISSING LINKS?

According to the evolution model there should be countless transitional forms showing the progression of life from one kind to another. *(Figure 60.)* If random and undirected evolution occurred, permitting freedom for development in many different directions, then there should be obvious examples showing how this has taken place. The fossils embedded in the crust of the earth should show the record of the transition of life forms in the past. Also, if this theory is valid, we should be able to identify living things in the process of change from one kind to another.

It is true that many scientists have convinced the public of numerous examples in the fossil record of missing links. Science textbooks are full of proposals, supposedly proving beyond a shadow of a doubt the existence of transitional forms. Often these proposals are nothing more than a combination of artistic imagination and some very inconclusive evidence.

The whale is often used by scientists as a example of evolution. Theory suggests that primitive mammalian ancestors lived on land before developing into marine dwelling creatures. It is proposed that the whale's ancestor had legs which later evolved into flippers. Over the past several years, evolutionists have made serious attempts to locate a fossil that would substantiate this theory. For example, in the *Science Digest*, November, 1980, there is an article on page 25 entitled, "Whales With Legs." The reader is shown an artist's drawing of a "whale-like" creature with legs and told the following:

*Not far from the Khyber pass in the arid Himalayan foothills of Pakistan, University of Michigan paleontologist Phillip Gingerich found a skull and several teeth, and came to the startling conclusion that they had belonged to an ancient walking whale. Gingerich*

*is returning to the Himalaya foothills this fall to find
more fossils so he can piece together a clearer picture of the whale's evolutionary history—he hopes
to find leg bones belonging to the whale species. "It
is possible that we will find some," he says, "but
we will be lucky if we do."*

There has never been a fossil found that would show that
whales had legs, yet drawings like the one shown with this
particular article leave the impression that organisms like this
do exist. *(Figure 61.)* Speculation of this nature can not be
classified as science and is certainly not adequate information to show transitional forms exist.

The giraffe is often used by evolutionists as a text book example of gradual change. The theory claims the long neck of
the giraffe developed as the environment selected out this
characteristic. The long neck was supposed to be an advan-
tage for reaching foliage that was higher in the trees. However,
there is an obvious flaw to this assumption. No one has ever
found a single fossil of a giraffe with a shorter neck.

## Archeopteryx

Another popular example of a proposed missing link is a
fossil named archeopteryx. *(Figure 62.)* This creature is claimed by most evolutionists to be the link that ties together the
bird family with the reptiles. The fossil indicated that this
creature had feathers, wings, and a beak. Other characteristics
archeopteryx exhibits, which have led paleontologists to seek
a tie with the reptiles, are the presence of teeth in its mouth
and claws on its wings.

These two characteristics do not prove archeopteryx has
evolved from reptiles. Birds like the ostrich have claws on
their wings and they are obviously classified as birds. Although
there are no living birds with teeth in their mouths, there are
many examples of birds in the fossil record that have teeth.
Some reptiles have teeth, and some do not, so this

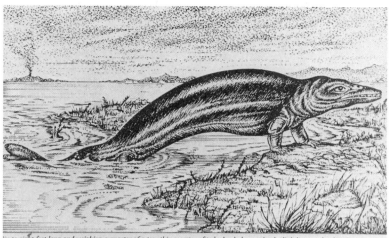

ix to eight feet long and weighing a quarter of a ton, this ancestor of today's whale may be the link between land and sea mamma

*Figure 61:*
*Artists' drawings are often used as proof that evolution is a fact. This example from Science Digest, November, 1980, shows that artwork can often reflect wild imagination rather than sound, observable evidence.*

characteristic should not be particularly important in distinguishing birds from reptiles.

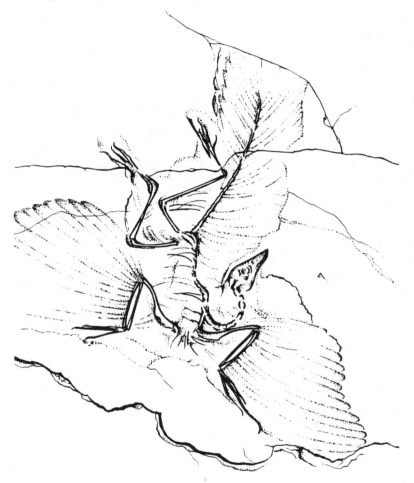

*Figure 62:*
*Many evolutionists claim that archeopteryx is a perfect example of a fossil demonstrating the transition between one kind of life and another. It is alleged to be a link between birds and reptiles.*

If archeopteryx can be classified as a link between reptiles and birds as evolutionists claim, then the age for fossils of birds would have to be younger. However this is not the case. *Science News*, September 24, 1977, mentions a bird fossil that was found in Colorado. Dating of this particular specimen by radiometric techniques gave an age of over 140 million years old. This is as old or older than the proposed age for archeopteryx. By the evolutionists' own claim of radiometric dating, we see the impossibility of making the archeopteryx a missing link.

Let's stop for a moment and think of some of the incredible changes that would be required for the evolution of birds from animals such as the reptile kind. Scales would have to change and become feathers. Front legs would have to modify and become wings. The skeletal system would have to be modified and lightened. The body metabolism would have to change drastically in order to provide enough energy for flight. It seems rather impossible that all of these major changes could suddenly appear by chance.

Scientists have put forth numerous suggestions outlining the evolution of flight in birds. The following quotation taken out of *Science Year Book, 1980*, page 292, discusses this very subject:

> *Most paleontologists assumed that archeopteryx could fly, or at least glide from tree to tree. They assumed that the bird's ancestors learned to climb trees to escape from predators and to seek insect food. Once the bird was in the tree, feathers and wings evolved to aid in gliding from branch to branch.*

> *Paleontologist John H. Ostrum of Yale University in New Haven, Connecticut reported in January 1979, however, that archeopteryx learned to fly from the ground up, and not from the trees down. Carnivores ran along the ground chasing flying insects, which they nabbed with their teeth or their front legs. Longer*

> *feathers on the front legs evolved to act as an insect*
> *net, and so the legs became wings. Then they used*
> *the wings to make flapping leaps after insects.*

It is obvious these two suggestions for the origin of bird flight made by two scientists are nothing more than pure speculation and humorous imagination which borders the ridiculous. It takes a great deal of imagination to consider these theories as being the least bit logical. Did flight evolve by some gradual process of evolution over millions of years of time, or was it designed by a Creator?

## Coelocanth

For years the coelocanth was claimed to be a link between the fish and the amphibian. *(Figure 63.)*

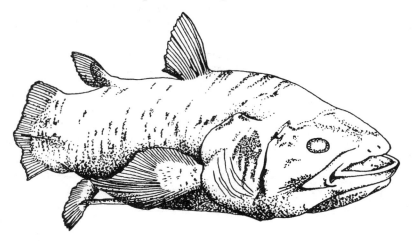

*Figure 63:*
*The coelocanth is often cited as a transitional form of life linking amphibians with fish. Evolutionists believed that it became extinct over 70 million years ago, until a living specimen was caught in 1939.*

Evolutionists claimed this creature had become extinct approximately 90 million years ago. Because of this assumption, the coelocanth was often used as an index fossil for dating layers of the earth. Whenever a coelocanth fossil was found it was immediately determined that the layer it was found in had to be at least 90 million years old.

However, in 1939 a living coelocanth was caught off the coast of Madagascar near Africa. Since then many of these creatures have been observed. Obviously, the coelocanth can no longer be used as an index fossil to date the layers of the earth. No longer can it be cited as an example of a fossil that shows the evolution of life from one kind to another.

## Horse Evolution

Nearly every textbook on the subject of evolution has a chart showing the documented evolution of the modern day horse from a four-toed, rabbit-size creature over millions of years of time. *(Figure 64.)* The chart is assembled from fossils found in India, South America, North America, and Europe, then arranged in a neat sequential order of size from the smallest to the largest. Certainly, there is a great deal of speculation involved in the formation of such a chart. There is no proof whatsoever that one member of the chart has evolved into another.

In some parts of the world the chart is found in an upside down reverse order. For example, Dr. Duanne Gish mentions in the September, 1980 issue of *Impact* that in South America, the so called younger members of the chart are found in older geological layers, and the older members of the chart are found in younger geological layers.

Today, many scientists who are committed evolutionists do not accept the scientific validity of the chart depicting the evolution of the horse. In spite of this, the chart continues to be used in science books as factual proof for the theory of evolution.

*Figure 64:*
*Evolutionists claim the development of the modern horse can*
*be traced back over millions of years of time to a creature*
*the size of a rabbit. The evidence used to substantiate this posi-*
*tion appears rather questionable.*

## Monkey to Man

When the subject of missing links is discussed, one immediately thinks of the missing links proposed that supposedly tie together the monkey kind with the human kind. If the theory of evolution is correct, then there should be numerous links connecting these two kinds of life together.

What kind of evidence is there to show that monkey-like creatures have changed and become modern man? It is interesting to note that evolutionists start with the assumption man has evolved from the ape, then attempt to assemble the evidence in order to support their case. *(Figure 65.)* Textbooks and other publications written about the subject of the origin and history of man are often filled with artwork illustrating primitive brute-like creatures. Are these drawings based on sound scientific evidence or are they nothing more than speculation and vivid imagination of the artist?

To date, there has never been a fossil found to indicate a link in the lineage of man from the ape. Fossils are either pure ape or pure man. Over the past several decades evolutionists have offered numerous links in the lineage of man. Upon close examination, however, these have proven to be based on either inadequate or outright fraudulant evidence. One such example, Nebraska Man, was used for years as proof for the evolution of man from the ape. This so called link was reconstructed from a single tooth, which was later determined to be the tooth of an extinct pig.

Most people who accept the biblical premise of creation are not aware of one of the major objectives behind the teaching of evolution and the view that man has developed from the monkey. The theory advocates that man is on a pathway of evolution to a higher, more complex dimension of understanding and awareness. The theory rejects God as the Creator and sustainer of life. Such a theory is at the very heart of the humanist religious movement of our day.

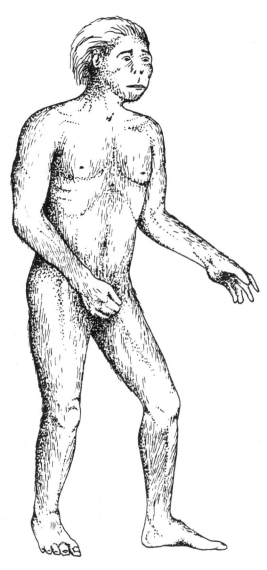

*Figure 65:*
*Textbook drawings attempting to reconstruct the appearance*
*of ancient man are often nothing more than artistic specula-*
*tion and are not based on sound scientific evidence.*

# GEOLOGY AND THE FOSSIL RECORD

## THE GEOLOGICAL COLUMN

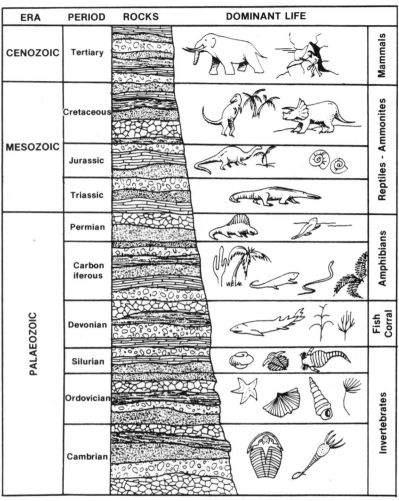

*Figure 66:*
*The geological column is a textbook chart found in most books dealing with the subjects of biology and geology. It proposes to show the development of living creatures in the layers of the earth in an order from simple to complex.*

# GEOLOGY AND THE GEOLOGICAL COLUMN

In the previous section of this book, we looked at some of the major ideas that the evolutionary theory is founded upon. As we could see, each principle of the evolution model was based on speculative assumption and not on sound, observable, factual information.

Another important principle of the theory of evolution is based on the science of geology. Geology deals with the study of the earth and the rocks from which it is composed, the changes which the earth has undergone, and the changes it is undergoing. Historically, the study of geology began with the understanding that the earth's physical features had been shaped by sudden global catastrophic events such as floods, earthquakes, and volcanic eruptions. This idea was replaced by the theory of uniformitarianism, which suggested the geological features of the earth could be explained by very gradual environmental forces taking place over long periods of time.

Many scientists consider geology the strongest proof for the evolution theory. Evolutionary textbooks written on the subject of the origin and history of the earth almost always have an illustration of the geological column included in them. *(Figure 66.)* The concept has become so well accepted by geologists that it is no longer considered a theory but a fact.

The foundational principle for the geological column is based on the assumption the earth is billions of years old. As we have previously mentioned, the idea that the earth's geological features were formed as a result of gradual processes taking place over long periods of time rather than by a mechanism of catastrophe was first proposed by men who were attempting to discredit the authenticity of the Bible.

The geological column is an attempt made by the evolutionist to provide a model to explain the numerous layers or strata found in the crust of the earth. Evolution teaches that the layers of the earth were deposited over millions and millions of years of time by gradual uniform processes. *(Figure 67.)* In essence, the theory of uniformitarianism states that the processes of erosion, sedimentation, and volcanic activity took place in the past at the same rate it occurs today.

*Figure 67:*
*The earth's surface is made up of layers called strata. A layer may range in thickness from a few inches to thousands of feet. Evolution theory accepts that deposition of these layers took place by uniform gradual processes over extremely long periods of time.*

Typical textbook illustrations of the geological column usually depict the layers or strata of the earth on the left side of the chart arranged in an orderly sequence with the oldest layers at the bottom and the youngest layers at the top. Each strata is given a designated name and assigned an age.

Associated with this concept of gradual deposition of the layers of the earth over long periods of time is the belief that living things were evolving upon the earth at the same time as the layers were being formed. According to the theory of evolution, there was a continual progression and development of life taking place in the direction from simple to complex. Non-living building blocks randomly formed single celled organisms which randomly developed into multicellular plants or multicellular animals. Animals without backbones randomly developed into fish; fish became four-legged amphibians; then amphibians eventually developed into reptiles. Reptiles with scales developed into birds or fur-bearing mammals. Mammals eventually walked upright and developed into apes, and finally into humans.

The evolution theory further deduces that a record of the organisms that lived in the past should be found preserved in the layers of the earth in a sequential record of increasing complexity. Simpler forms of life should be found in older layers deeper in the earth's crust while more advanced forms should be found in younger layers closer to the earth's surface.

## Serious Problems in Using the Geological Column

In order to better understand the significance of the geological column and how it is used, let us examine it in more detail. If the geological column can be classified as an acceptable scientific model, then it should be able to stand the test of being verified by the observable evidence.

It is important to realize that the ages assigned to the various strata making up the column were determined over 150 years ago and were based on nothing more than pure assumption and speculation. No one can prove scientifically how long a period of time was required for a particular layer to be laid down in the past. Any amount of time chosen for the formation of such a layer has to be based on an assumption that can not be tested.

Another observation which causes one to question the hypothetical geological column is the precise and well defined boundaries that always exist between strata. If the theory of uniformitarianism is correct, certainly one would expect a gradual blending of one layer into the next.

Are there other important reasons for questioning the validity of the geological column? The proposed sequence of geological layers laid down in an order from the oldest to the youngest can not be found anywhere in the real world. No geologist has been able to find a single location on earth where there is a complete sequence of the strata which have been laid down in the same order as depicted by the textbook charts.

## Using the Geological Column to Date Fossils

A farmer who did not have access to a scale wanted to determine the weight of a pig. In order to do so, he constructed a balancing device using a plank and a saw-horse. *(Figure 68.)* On one end of the plank he secured the pig. Then he located a large stone just the right weight that would exactly balance the pig. He then estimated the weight of the rock. Because the farmer believed the estimation of the weight of the rock was accurate, he then determined the weight of the pig. Confident that he had arrived at an accurate weight for the pig, he further assumed he had arrived at an accurate weight for the rock.

It does not take a great scientific mind to see the error that the farmer made as he attempted to determine the weight of his pig. It is obvious that it is impossible to set up an accurate system of measuring weight based on an assumption dependent on something which is unknown. Evolutionists who have thought through this simple illustration of circular reasoning

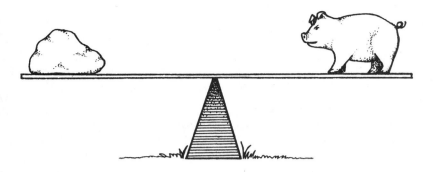

*Figure 68:*
*The above illustration shows how a farmer incorrectly weighed a pig. If the weight of the rock on the left was determined by an assumption, the weight of the pig can not be determined with any degree of accuracy.*

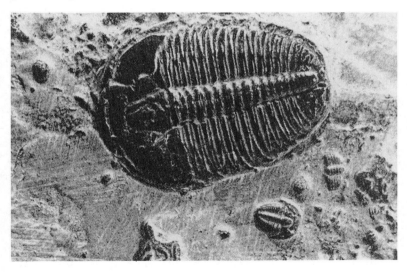

*Figure 69:*
*A trilobite is an extinct form of life found in the fossil record. Even though this organism has complex eyes, evolutionists have chosen the trilobite as a primitive form of multicellular life, thus placing it at the bottom of the geological chart.*

find it extremely humorous, and of course very unscientific. The method in which the geological time scale was constructed and the way that it is used for dating fossils and the layers of the earth follows the same pattern of unreliable assumptions used by the farmer who attempted to weigh his pig.

To the average person who has a trust and respect for the science of geology, dating procedures are unquestionably accepted as absolute and true. The acceptance of the geological column over the past several decades by geologists has established a method for dating the layers of the earth and the fossils. Very few have actually investigated the history behind the formation of the geological column, nor have they considered how the column is used to establish the proposed ages of various fossil finds.

Nearly everyone is aware of fossil discoveries found in certain areas and reported by the media. Very often the ages of the fossils are published immediately after they have been found, long before it would have been possible to use radioactive dating techniques to determine an age. Most people accept these dates for the age of the fossil as being very accurate and reliable without even questioning how they were determined.

In order to better understand how the geological column is used to date fossils, let us consider the following example. Suppose that one day while you were on a fossil hunting expedition you came across a well-preserved specimen of a trilobite embedded in a layer of rock. *(Figure 69.)* In an attempt to determine the age of the fossil, you chiseled the trilobite out of the rock and took it to a geologist for examination. The geologist, without knowing anything more about the fossil or the layer of rock in which it was found, and without using a radiometric dating technique, would be able to immediately tell you the age of the trilobite. How would this be possible? *(Figure 70.)*

In order for a geologist to make an assessment of the age of any fossil, he must totally rely on the assumptions that were

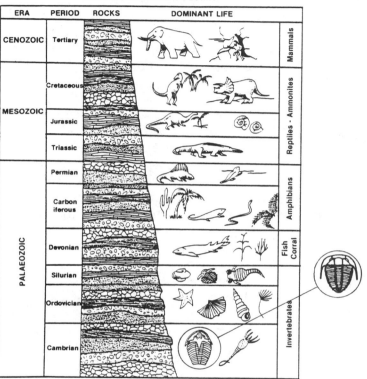

**Figure 70:**
*The geological chart is often used by evolutionists to determine the age of a fossil. In the above example, the age of a trilobite fossil is established by simply using the theoretical dates that were assigned to the geological column when it was first proposed over 150 years ago.*

proposed in the formation of the geological column. The age
of the fossils preserved in the numerous layers of the earth's
crust and the proposed sequence of evolutionary development
were assumed by the proponents of the theory of evolution
approximately one hundred and fifty years ago. Those dates
are still used and accepted as absolute scientific fact to this
present day. The following statement taken from *Science Year
Book 1980,* page 200, clarifies this point:

> *Scientists before Darwin also knew that rocks from
> different time periods in the geological past contained
> different kinds of fossils, and they had worked out
> the basic sequence of life remarkably well. In fact
> geologists still use the time scale that was established,
> years before Darwin wrote, dividing the earth into
> eras, periods, and epochs that lasted millions of
> years. These time periods were defined by the kinds
> of fossils found in each period.*

Thus, given the assumption that the various time periods
and their associated fossils are accurate, a geologist feels he
is capable of assessing the age of any fossil with confidence.
In the case of a trilobite fossil, a geologist would immediately suggest this organism lived in a period of time between 600
and 230 million years ago. Once you have placed your trust
in the time scale for the various eras of the geological column, any other fossil can be dated as well.

The geological column can not only be used to date fossils,
but it can also be used to assess the age of the various layers
of the earth. Suppose you have discovered a layer of the earth
and you were interested in finding out how many years ago
the layer was formed. Once again, the geological column
would be used to determine the age of the layer. A geologist
would be able to estimate the approximate age of the layer
by examining the layer and determining what kind of fossils
were present.

For example, suppose a thick layer of volcanic ash material was exposed by a ravine which cut through the top soil by a flash flood. In order for a geologist to assess how long ago the volcanic ash layer had been deposited, it would be necessary to dig through the layer until some kind of fossil remains were found. In this particular situation, the excavation revealed the fossil fragments of a dinosaur. A geologist would immediately have the information required to date the layer. According to the geological chart, it is assumed the dinosaur era existed between 200 to 65 million years ago, thus making the layer in question of that same approximate age.

As we have looked at these two examples showing how the geological chart can be used to date fossils and layers, it is apparent there is a conflict that can not be resolved. In the first case, we saw that the chart was used to date a fossil according to the assumed age of the particular layer it was found in. In the second example, the age of a particular layer was established by assigning a date based on the assumed age of the fossil found in the layer. These two examples illustrate the circular reasoning which occurs in the dating process as related to the geological chart.

First, we must recognize that all of the ages and time periods given on the chart are based on an assumption. Second, fossils are dated by the assumed age of the layers in which they are found, and conversely, layers are dated by the assumed age of the fossils contained in the layers. This process of circular reasoning is exactly the same kind of reasoning that the farmer used to weigh his pig.

If one is truly honest with the evidence, it is obvious that circular reasoning does not belong in the realm of science, yet this method is used over and over again as if it were an absolute scientific fact. Scientists who refute the validity of the geological column and its use for assessing the age of fossils and layers are looked upon by the secular world as heretics and religious fools. Certainly, it is time the evolutionary concept of the geological column was challenged and re-examined with an open mind.

# GEOLOGY AND THE
# OBSERVABLE EVIDENCE

Throughout this book we have been constantly looking at the claims made by the two opposing models for the origin and history of the earth—evolution and creation. After examining these claims we have then turned to the observable evidence to see which of the two models appears to be the most credible.

The creation model section of this book dealt with an area which gave an overview of what the Bible states the original earth was like. We mentioned how the original earth was much different from the earth as we know it today. Subtropical life flourished under a greenhouse environment from pole to pole. Varieties of life were not only larger and more vigorous, but there were many more kinds of life than exist today.

According to the Scriptures, the original earth experienced a cataclysmic event of global proportions at the time of the Noahic flood. Mass extinctions occurred as a result of catastrophic events which affected the entire planet. Volcanic eruptions, cosmic fallout, massive deposition of water and ice, tidal wave activity, and geological upheavals rapidly destroyed life. The biblical premise predicts that life should be found in the various stratas of the earth revealing the evidence of catastrophic deposition. According to the creation model, life should be found scrambled together, in no specific order, often mixed with volcanic debris, and laid down in flood deposited horizontal layers.

If these events occurred in the past as the Bible states they have, then there must certainly be evidence to be observed. Examination of the observable evidence from around the world will help us to evaluate whether or not the creation model is true. Once again we will see that what the Bible states has taken place in the past can be proven by the geological layers and the fossils they contain.

## The Burgess Shale Fossil Bed

The Burgess Shale fossil bed near Field, British Columbia, Canada, has been described as one of the richest fossil bearing locations in the world. The Burgess Shale site is particularly rich in trilobite fossils, a form of life that was supposed to have flourished during the so-called Cambrian period of time, alleged to have occurred half a billion years ago.

Along with the trilobites found in this location are numerous other strange looking animals and plants which have been described as creatures looking like something out of science fiction. An article written in the *Vancouver Sun,* October 9, 1980, called "The Way We Were Written In Stone," describes the amazing structural complexity of the fossilized remains of some of the creatures found in this location. Many of the organisms found there are so bizarre in their appearance that paleontologists have not even attempted to connect them to any family of modern animals.

The sudden profusion of so many highly advanced forms of life that appear suddenly in the fossil record has caused some scientists to reconsider their views on how evolution has occurred. The article states the opinion of Harry Whittington of Cambridge University in England, who has done extensive studies of the Burgess fossils:

> *The textbook evolutionary tree, with everything traced back to a few common ancestors, is inaccurate. Instead, evolution is a thicket, with a rich diversity of species in the remote past, many of them ultimately unsuccessful.*

Not only is the sudden appearance of so many complex forms of life a mystery, but the very reason for their preservation in such minute detail in a tropical-like environment of the past needs to be explained as well. Jim Aitken of the Canadian Geological Survey in Calgary, Alberta, is a geologist who has collected specimens from the Burgess location. He explains in this same article how evolutionists believe the Burgess fossils were formed.

> *Back in the so-called middle Cambrian period, the earth spun about an axis that had the north pole in the Pacific Ocean, and Field, in tropical or sub-tropical latitudes. There was no trace of British Columbia's present mountains. A warm ocean lapped the western border of Saskatchewan. Near Field there was an offshore reef that brushed the surface of the sea, then abruptly dropped 150 meters to the seabed. Fine mud collected in the sloping beds against the bottom of the reef, where the creatures of the Burgess Shale thrived.*
>
> *But from time to time disaster struck this marine community. The mud slopes were unstable. A small underwater avalanche of mud would occur, sweeping up plants and animals and burying them at a lower depth. Normally, scavengers and decay would quickly destroy the buried bodies, leaving only a few stems and shells to be preserved in the fossil record. But some of the avalanches occurred in a region where the water was low in oxygen. Scavengers could not live there and decay was arrested. With time, the bodies were flattened and the minerals infiltrated the tissues because of the fineness of the mud and the smallest details were preserved.*

The conventional explanation for the Burgess Shale fossil bed is based upon the premise that living organisms are the product of the process of evolution occurring over long periods of time. The many different kinds of life forms, and the incredible design and complexity revealed by the fossils preserved there, has caused evolutionists themselves to question some of their long-held, cherished ideas about how evolution supposedly has taken place.

The presence of the trilobite, which has always been classified as the most primitive form of multicellular life along with the presence of many other complex forms of multicellular life, challenges the idea of the existence of an orderly sequence of life as proposed by the geological column. In other words, the common textbook chart showing the evolution of life as a tree with all present life forms traced back to a few common ancestors does not agree with the evidence. *(Figure 71.)* The Burgess Shale reveals the appearance of multiplied forms of complex life along with the trilobite. This evidence agrees completely with the biblical premise.

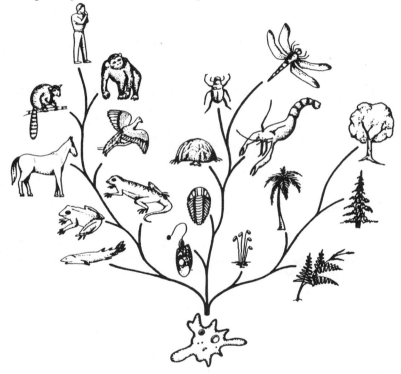

*Figure 71:*
*One of the major assumptions of the evolutionary model is that all forms of life can be traced back to a few common ancestors. The observable evidence reveals that multiplied forms of complex life appear on the scene at the same time.*

The other interesting aspect of the fossil bed at Field, British Columbia, is the apparent relationship of a tropical type environment which existed at the time fossilization took place. Evolutionists have attempted to explain the change that took place in the climate from the remote past to the present day by stating the earth's geographic poles have shifted position. However, as we have already pointed out by looking at fossil evidence of many different kinds of life from all over the world, tropical or subtropical environments occurred on a global basis. Once again it would appear that the biblical concept of an original canopied earth would adequately explain the reason for the climatic difference from the past to the present.

The mechanism for fossilization of life on a localized basis, explained by the reasoning from the uniformitarian model, can also be questioned in light of the biblical model for the origin and history of the earth. The Bible suggests that all kinds of perfected life which existed in a tropical like environment were destroyed by a global cataclysmic event involving flood waters covering the entire earth. The fossil evidence indicates that rapid deposition and burial of life forms of all kinds appears to be the general rule rather than the exception.

## The Love Bone Bed

The Love Bone Bed, located 12 miles west of Gainsville, Florida, has become known as one of the richest sites for fossil exploration in North America. Excavation at this location, which took place from 1974 to 1981, has revealed over 100 species of vertebrates embedded in the earth's surface.

Scientists have excavated a site measuring 120 feet long by 60 feet wide and approximately 15 feet deep. This area, which is the size of an average gymnasium, has yielded over a million fossils. In some places of the excavation the fossilized remains are so tightly packed together that bone makes up over 50 percent of the deposit.

Many different kinds of animals from both marine and land habitats are represented. The remains of extinct sharks, whales, and manatees show the site was close to salt water, but fresh water fish and animals such as gar, alligators, and turtles indicate the presence of fresh water. Land animals that have been found there include snakes, rodents of various kinds, two species of raccoon, four species of wolves, a sabre-tooth cat, an elephant, a tapir, two species of rhinoceroses, seven kinds of horses, a llama, and three species of camels.

In order to understand the scrambling together of the many kinds of life from both land and water habitats, paleontologists offer the following explanation. Nine million years ago the sea level surrounding Florida was higher than it is today, creating a salt water marsh extending inland for 60 miles more than it is today. A fresh water stream flowed lazily into the salt water marsh. Around the bank of the stream was a forest interspersed with fresh water marshes. The Love Bone bed was supposedly a bend in the stream where fossils accumulated in the still water.

*Science And Mechanics* —Special Edition, 1981, page 108 and 109 has an article about the Love Bone Bed location called "Digging Up Florida's Past." In this article an interview is made with Dr. David Webb, a paleontologist with the Florida State Museum. Webb, who has directed the excavation, makes the following statement:

> *It's almost impossible to find 100 species of living vertebrates in any one place today. To find that many fossils is incredible. The concentration of bones is unbelievable, and that says that life must have been rich and productive in this location in the past. The climate looks to have been even more tropical and lush than Florida today. There are many unique species here, even a number of species not known to scientists from anywhere else. Many of the animals are like those out of the American tropics.*

The mass burial of so many varieties of life in such a concentrated area is exactly what one would expect if an event such as a global flood had occurred. The environmental tropical conditions present at the time the fossils were formed also agrees with the biblical model of a canopied earth. Once again, the physical observable evidence agrees with the Word of God.

## Kenya, Africa

A well known fossil of a human-like skull called Skull 1470 was found by Richard Leakey east of Lake Rudolf in Kenya, Africa, in August, 1972. The discovery of Skull 1470 triggered off a great deal of controversy amongst paleontologists, or scientists who attempt to trace the lineage of man back to the ape. *National Geographic,* June, 1973, in an article called "Skull 1470—New Clue To Earliest Man" on page 819, quotes Richard Leakey regarding the significance of the fossil:

> *Either we toss out this skull or we toss out our theories of early man. It simply fits no previous models of human beginnings. It leaves in ruins the notion that all early fossils can be arranged in an orderly sequence of evolutionary change.*

Controversy surrounded Skull 1470 because of its classification as belonging to the genus Homo, the same genus as modern human beings. Prior to the discovery of this particular skull, the earliest previous suggestion of the genus Homo had been a proposed 1.8 million year old creature called Homo habilis, found by Lewis Leakey in the Olduvai Gorge in Tanzania. Potassium argon dating of volcanic tuft in the layer surrounding Skull 1470 gave an age of approximately 2.8 million years to the fossil. Richard Leakey's discovery pushed back many anthropologists' estimates about the beginning date of human evolution by approximately another million years.

Another interesting thing about the find of Skull 1470 is the description of the environment present at the time the fossilization process took place. In this same article from *National Geographic*, Leakey describes the area as once being near a large fresh water lake fed by tropical streams. Leakey mentions that the wealth of other fossils found there indicated ''a picture of a vast green expanse teaming with game.'' He also suggests that the reason for the region's multilayered geological record is because of periods of ''frequent flooding and widespread volcanic activity.'' Once again, the biblical premise of a destruction of a tropical type environment by volcanic destruction and flood activity can be supported by the evidence.

Other revealing evidence associated with the find of Skull 1470 causes the honest observer to question the credibility of the evolutionary interpretation of the origin of modern man. On page 88 of the book *Origins*, written by Richard Leakey, mention is made of the discovery of a leg bone in the same area that Skull 1470 was found. The following statement is made:

> *Not long after the few scraps of bones were spotted that gave us 1470, John Harris, a paleontologist in the team, was examining the fossilized remains of an elephant being eroded from the ground, when, in the middle of the shattered pieces, he noticed sections of an almost complete thigh bone (femur) and the top and bottom parts of the lower leg (tibia and fibula) of a remarkably advanced hominid. When they were examined closely, there was practically no difference from modern human leg bones.*

Is it just possible that the leg bone and the fossil fragments called Skull 1470 could have belonged to a individual as human as we are today? Although the cranial capacity of the skull is only 800 cubic centimeters as compared to the average modern human cranium of approximately 1400 cubic centimeters, there is no way of knowing if the fossil skull was an adult at time of death.

The age of 2.8 million years assigned to the skull was determined by radiometric dating of volcanic material located in the surrounding area. Earlier in this book we looked at the reliability of the radiometric dating methods and found they were based upon some questionable assumptions. Can the evolutionist accept the age for Skull 1470 as one hundred percent accurate or is it possible this skull may have been buried in recent historical times? Once again, the biblical premise of the destruction of many kinds of life along with the human kind in the recent past fits well with the evidence that is seen in Kenya, Africa.

## The Asphalt Pit of La Brea

The La Brea asphalt pits, located in the midst of Los Angeles, California, are another example of the abundant preservation of many forms of life in the fossil record. The tar pits of La Brea are an outcropping of beds of petroleum shale that originate in northern California and extend for a distance of over 450 miles to Los Angeles and beyond.

The deposit containing the fossils consists of alluvium, a type of sedimentary material of sand and mud formed by the action of flowing water. Mixed together with the alluvial deposition is coarse sand, gravel, and asphalt. Since the La Brea asphalt pits were discovered, over one million well preserved fossils have been dug out of the layers of oil and tar. The animal remains, crowded together in an unbelievable agglomeration, include bears, sabretoothed tigers, giant wolves, llamas, camels, horses, giant ground sloths, bison, and birds.

In order to explain the presence of so many kinds of life found in the mud and asphalt, a theory has been proposed that the animals became entrapped in the tar when they came to this location for a drink, sank in it, and were permanently embedded when the tar hardened. It is suggested that as the animals were dying, their helpless cries were heard by other animals in the area, attracting them to the site and the same fate.

Immanuel Velikovsky, in his book *Earth In Upheaval*, page 61, tells about the presence of human skeletal remains at this location.

> *Separate bones of a human skeleton were also discovered in the asphalt of La Brea. The skull belonged to an Indian of the Ice Age, it is assumed. However, it does not show any deviation from the normal skull of Indians. The human bones were found in the asphalt, under the bones of a vulture of an extinct species. These finds suggest that the time when the human body was buried preceded the extinction of that species of vulture or at least coincided with it.*

The explanation for the presence of so many life forms might seem reasonable if the state of the bones in the tar pits did not reveal the ensnarement by violent circumstances. The majority of the skeletons are not found connected together but are broken, mashed, contorted, and scrambled together, such as could have never happened gradually as the theory suggests. It would seem more logical to accept that animals along with humans were buried in a mass grave which was the result of a catastrophic deposition involving flood activity and bitumenous material falling from the heavens. Such a catastrophe is in keeping with the biblical model.

## The Siwalik Hills

The Siwalik Hills are located at the southern base of the Himalaya mountain range. The Himalayas, noted for being the highest mountain range in the world, rise like a fifteen hundred mile wall at the northern border of India. Many of the peaks of the Himalayas tower over 20,000 feet. Mount Everest, the world's highest peak, is located in this range.

During the nineteenth century, scientists who climbed the

slopes of the Himalaya Mountains were dismayed to find the evidence of many forms of marine organisms such as fish and clams in a fossilized condition. According to the common geological assumption, it is believed the great mountain range is the result of the uplift of an ancient sea bed.

The Siwalik Hills are better known as the foothills of the Himalayas. Situated north of Delhi, India, they extend for several hundred miles and are three thousand to four thousand feet in height. The extremely rich fossil beds found there have drawn attention from scientists from all over the world. Animal bones of numerous species of animals both living and extinct are found in amazing profusion. In the book *Earth In Upheaval*, written by Immanuel Velikovsky, the following statement is made:

> *The Siwalik Hills are stocked with animals of so many and such varied species that the animal world of today seems impoverished by comparison. It looks as though all the animals have invaded the world at one time.*

Other scientists who have observed the numerous kinds of life scrambled together in this massive burial ground have had difficulty in trying to find an explanation. D. N. Wadia, on page 268 of his book *Geology of India*, states:

> *The sudden bursting on the stage of such a varied population of herbivores (plant eaters), carnivores (meat eaters), rodents, and of primates, the highest order of mammals, must be regarded as a most remarkable instance of rapid evolution of species.*

The tremendous accumulation of numerous kinds of fossils located in the Siwalik Hills is not just a localized phenomenon. Thirteen hundred miles further east in central Burma, a layer estimated at over 10,000 feet thick contains hundreds of different kinds of fossilized life. Two fossil-rich zones are separated by approximately 4000 feet of sand. The upper fossil bed, similar to the Siwalik deposits, is jammed full of animals including the mastadon, hippopotamus, and ox. Other sedimentary layers found beneath are loaded with large quantities of fossilized wood. Hundreds of thousands of entire tree trunks and logs embedded in the sandstone suggest that heavily forested areas were quickly stripped from their natural habitat and buried under catastrophic conditions.

What was the agent that caused the burial and preservation of so many forms of life? Certainly nothing like this can be observed occurring in the world today. Is it reasonable to hold firm to the theory that uniform, gradual processes were the cause? Once again, the biblical model for the catastrophic history of the earth can be confirmed by the observable evidence.

*Figure 72:*
*Fossils show what life was like in the past.*

# FOSSILIZATION

One of the major areas of discussion revealing the extreme contrast existing between the creation and evolution models and the history of the earth is the question of how the process of fossilization has occurred. Were fossils formed by gradual events that occurred over long periods of time or were they formed as the result of a catastrophic deposition that occurred by sudden global events?

Fossils are the record or the remains of plants and animals living in the past. *(Figure 72.)*

Fossils are found throughout the world in the various layers of the earth showing the structure of many forms of life. Fossils may be whole organisms frozen in ice, a bone or tooth hardened by minerals, an insect encased in amber, the form of a footprint, or the impression of a leaf. Usually, it is only the harder parts of the organism such as the skeleton that is preserved, but occasionally softer tissues are fossilized as well.

The process of fossilization is often described as a mystery. No one has been able to duplicate the mineralization process in the laboratory. Most explanations proposed by evolutionists are based upon gradual deposition of life over long periods of time by sedimentary processes. The common explanation which usually appears in geology textbooks is as follows. The mineralization process takes place as water saturated in minerals gradually migrates through the tissues, dissolving the organic material and replacing it with the inorganic silica-based molecules from the water. Prints of thin objects, such as leaves and feathers, are said to have been formed by impressions made in soft mud which later hardened into stone. Animals that have been found fully preserved in a frozen condition are said to have occurred by an isolated accidental situation, with no mention of sudden change in climatic or environmental conditions.

In order to better understand the process that may have

occurred to preserve a record of fossilized life in the past, let's look at several possibilities. One obvious observation to be made is that living things which die today decompose rather than change from organic into stone. For example, today when a fish dies in the water it soon floats to the surface and begins to decompose bit by bit, eventually falling apart before any trace of its structure is left permanently recorded. Animals which die on the land are either eaten by predators or quickly broken down by the process of decomposition. Dying plants, leaves, stems, and even entire trees are broken down and decomposed in short periods of time. How did the process of fossilization occur in the past?

The most obvious explanation for the preservation of fossil evidence is that life must have been rapidly buried under vast volumes of catastrophic deposition. Extremely high temperatures and pressures would have been important factors in the fossilization process. Sedimentary layers would not have been formed over millions of years by gradual deposition, but could have resulted from sudden burial by tidal activity, massive rearrangement of the land, and volcanic activity all occurring on a global basis.

The fossil record is loaded with examples confirming a catastrophic event of global proportions occurred in the past. As we have already pointed out throughout this book, fossil beds all over the world indicate that living organisms of every kind of life appear in the layers of the earth as if they were suddenly caught and destroyed while they were alive. They have not died natural deaths and then gradually been buried. In order to develop this point, let's look at some further examples.

## Fossilization of Fish

The skeletal remains of thousands of different varieties of fish are found preserved in the fossil record in every part of the world. In order to explain the existence of water dwelling organisms in regions where water does not exist today, geologists have proposed the idea that over millions of years of time great land masses have gradually sunk below sea level and allowed the sea to flood the land. Following this process, again over millions of years of time, land masses are said to have risen above the sea level. Left behind is the evidence of fossilized marine organisms that have died. Evolutionary geologists would claim these have been gradually covered over by the natural process of sedimentation.

This explanation for the process of fossilization leaves a number of questions which need to be answered. The delicate and intricate structures revealed by many of these fossilized marine organisms, further substantiates the idea that preservation of such detail must have been associated with short periods of time. In fact, countless fossils of fish all over the world reveal that death occurred in a split second of time as the creature was caught suddenly in a position of terror.

One such example clearly illustrates massive quantities of marine organisms have suffered the fate of violent death. Evidence can be found in a location known as The Red Sandstone, an area comprising half the country of Scotland. This region has been described by observers as an aquatic graveyard with thousands of different localities disclosing the same scene of destruction. The red sandstone deposit, which covers an area of approximately ten thousand square miles and over 150 feet in thickness, screams with the evidence of wide-scale catastrophe. Fossilized fish are found there contorted into abnormal shapes. In many instances the tail is bent around to the head, and spines are sticking straight out as if the fish had died in a convulsion.

The identical picture can be found in northern Italy. Evidence there would indicate vast quantities of fish perished suddenly. Fossilized skeletons of fish are found by the thousands in the strata of calcareous slate. In most cases the skeletons are complete and tightly packed together. Many fossils have been preserved with traces of the color of their skin impregnated into the surrounding material, indicating that deposition had occurred before decomposition of the softer tissues could occur.

## Rapid Burial of Clams

Another good example of the rapid burial of marine organisms can be illustrated by the numerous clams all over the world that are found fossilized with their valves shut. When a clam dies, only a few hours elapse before the two halves of the shell begin to open or separate. Clams found with their valves shut would certainly indicate they had been buried alive. One of the best examples of clams found in this condition are fossil clams we have observed near Halkirk, Alberta, Canada. *(Figure 73.)*

*Figure 73:*
*Numerous fossilized clams are found near Halkirk, Alberta embedded in ironstone material. The valves of the clams are closed, indicating the process of fossilization must have occurred in a very short period of time.*

Many of these clams are encased in sheets of ironstone, which appears to have flowed in a molten condition over the clams at their time of death.

In other locations millions of marine-dwelling creatures are preserved in hot molten rock which has poured out upon the ocean floor. The biblical account of the Noahic flood explains why this has occurred. When the "fountains of the deep" broke up, volcanic eruptions occurred all over the surface of the earth, including land masses and ocean beds.

## Fossil Sharks

One final example of the rapid burial of marine organisms by catastrophic deposition can be illustrated by fossil sharks found in the rock layers of Ohio. Sharks of many different sizes are found in strata hundreds of feet thick. The remains of these creatures indicate they died in a natural swimming position with the belly down. The weight of the mud piled on top of them has squashed them to the thickness of a quarter of an inch or less. How could such an event have taken place by gradual uniform processes over long periods of time? Only an event like the global flood account in the Bible can properly give us a model suitable for analyzing the observable evidence.

## Fossilized Land Living Plants and Animals

Today, when a plant or animal dies, in a short period of time the tissues of the organism begin to decompose, are removed by predators, or broken down by microbial action. As previously mentioned, the evolutionary concept is that fossils are the remains of organisms which have died in the distant past under natural conditions and have been covered over by a gradual process of sedimentation. However, when the observable evidence is examined, countless fossils representing land-dwelling organisms which have lived in the past indicate this explanation for the mechanism of fossilization

ation needs to be seriously challenged.

The fossil record is loaded with examples which indicate living organisms were buried alive in massive burial grounds, and that the fossilization process took place almost immediately. If the uniformitarian premise that the present is the key to understanding the past is valid, then we should be able to point to processes occurring today to explain the vast extinctions of life which have occurred in the past. Let's examine examples of fossilized life from several locations around the world, attempting to evaluate whether the fossilization process occurred gradually or if it was sudden and catastrophic.

## Petrified Wood and Leaf Impressions

Pieces of wood that have been turned from organic material into stone, commonly called petrified wood, are one of the most common features of the fossil record. Close examination of petrified wood often reveals detailed structure such as annual growth rings. The petrification process is often described as a mystery by most geologists because it is not understood what caused the process to occur in the past nor is it understood why it is not occurring today. Even more mysterious is the presence of fossilized remains of softer plant tissues like leaves. The fossil record is loaded with examples of leaves which reveal minute structures of leaf venation and cellular detail.

One example of an area where an abundance of fossils can be found revealing the preservation of soft tissues of plants and animals is Drumheller, Alberta, Canada. The Drumheller badlands are made up of layers of volcanic ash and mud intermingled with coal seams that have been laid down in the past. Evolutionists believe the layers represent deposition which occurred over millions of years of time. This area has become famous world over for the remains of fossilized dinosaurs.

Interspersed throughout the many layers of deposition at Drumheller are petrified trees, fossilized marine organisms, clams and oysters, and pieces of petrified wood. Chunks of ironstone material are found throughout the layers, which almost always contain some form of fossilized life. *(Figure 75.)*

*Figure 74:*
*Chunks of ironstone material are commonly found throughout the volcanic layers at Drumheller, Alberta. Conventional geological theory suggests the ironstone chunks were formed over long periods of time by the gradual migration of minute iron particles.*

*Figure 75:*
*Ironstone material found in the ash layers at Drumheller often contains the fossilized remains of plants and animals.*

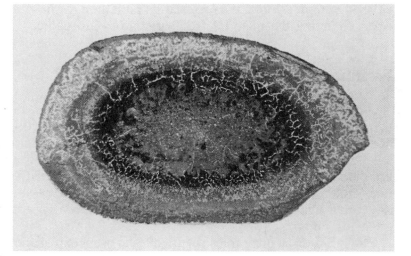

*Figure 76:*
*Examination of the ironstone material by researchers has shown that heat was definitely involved in the formation process of these rocks.*

Conventional explanations for the formation of the ironstone attempt to explain its origin by the gradual process of molecular migration. However, close examination of the ironstone material reveals perfect impressions of leaves, preservation of chunks of wood and other plant tissues. *(Figure 75.)* One chunk of ironstone that we observed at this location showed the perfect impression of a dragonfly wing. Obviously, the process that caused the preservation of these minute structural details could not have taken place over a long period of time, as suggested by uniformitarian geology. Analysis of the ironstone by atomic research scientists has shown the rocks were formed by heat and not by the process of molecular migration. *(Figure 76.)*

The biblical model offers a more logical explanation for the presence of the ironstone. During the time of the flood when layers of volcanic ash and mud were being laid down by tidal wave activity, molten brimstone material was falling from the heavens. This activity is described as "the windows of heaven" being opened (Genesis 7:11). Hot molten material falling from the heavens would fall on organic material, leaving either the impression of the material that it fell on, or in some cases changing the material from organic to inorganic.

## Fossilized Trees

Other locations around the world are famous for the petrification of entire trees. The Petrified Forest, located in northeastern Arizona, contains some of the largest petrified logs found anywhere in the world. *(Figure 77.)* Some of these great trees are over two hundred feet in length. The petrified trees are found in hundreds of feet of flood-deposited volcanic ash, often tightly packed together to give the appearance of great log jams.

How were these great trees petrified? The usual explanation given is that millions of years ago this area was a swampy location traversed by streams and rivers. It is claimed that as these rivers deposited their loads of sediment, and as the shifting streams moved sand, mud, and volcanic ash from place to place, thousands of logs, bones, and other pieces of plants and animals were gradually buried and fossilized.

Such a theory does not adequately explain the evidence. Rivers and streams that deposit sediments today do not provide the necessary conditions for the fossilization process, nor do they provide the mechanism for such wide-scale destruction which appears to have happened in this location in the past. The massive volumes of flood-deposited volcanic ash present at the Petrified Forest appear to have been the product of volcanic activity that must have occurred on a much larger scale than happens today. The conditions responsible for the petrification of these huge trees would more likely have been associated with a large-scale catastrophe of global proportions just as the Bible describes.

Another location where petrified trees are found in catastrophic deposition is at Yellowstone National Park, in the northern United States. The trees have been covered over by volcanic brecia at some time in the past, and fossilized to the level which they had been covered. In this region trees no longer grow to the size of their fossilized ancestors. *(Figure 78.)* Obviously, the destruction of the trees and the process which caused them to fossilize must have been sudden and very devastating.

## Polystrate Fossils

Other evidence which indicates rapid burial has played an important part in the fossilization process are trees which are found embedded in more than one layer or strata of the earth. A fossil of this nature is called a polystrate fossil.

An example of a polystrate tree is a fossil found in a Tennessee coal bed, shown in an article called, "Will Coal Be Tomorrow's Black Gold," on page 245 of the August, 1975, issue of *National Geographic. (Figure 79.)* The photograph shows the trunk of a large tree embedded in a coal seam. The tree continues to rise vertically through twelve feet of sandstone. Conventional geology would explain the coal formation and the sandstone layer by stating that uniform processes laid down these layers over millions of years of time. The presence of the tree through both of these layers, however, clearly indicates the deposition of the layers must have occurred in a very short period of time.

*Figure 77:*
*Huge trees are found in the Petrified Forest in Arizona that have been turned from living material into stone. The fossilized trees are found in hundreds of feet of volcanic ash. What kind of an event caused their destruction?*

*Figure 78:*
*The fossilized remains of huge trees stand in a vertical posi-*
*tion on the slopes of a mountain in Yellowstone National Park.*
*These trees appear to have been fossilized in the depth they*
*had been covered by volcanic brecia.*

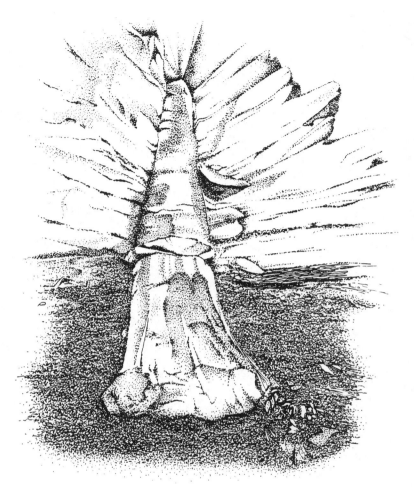

*Figure 79:*
*The drawing illustrates a petrified tree found in Tennessee.*
*The bottom part of the tree is embedded in a layer of coal.*
*The upper part of the tree is embedded in limestone.*

## Destruction of Dinosaurs

There are many examples of animal fossils which glaringly reveal a sudden catastrophic event was responsible for their demise. For example, it is not uncommon to find dinosaur fossils in positions that suggest sudden, violent death. Some have been uncovered in flood deposits with neck and tail broken, their bodies oriented with the flow of the water which laid them down. Duck-billed dinosaurs have been excavated in swimming positions buried in layers of volcanic ash and mud. *(Figure 80.)*

*Figure 80:*
*The fossilized remains of entire dinosaur skeletons are often discovered in the layers of volcanic ash near Drumheller, Alberta. It seems reasonable to suggest that the burial of these huge reptiles must have been sudden and catastrophic.*

Evolutionists have had to devise elaborate theories in order to explain why animals that are not aquatic should have died violently in water. Far too many specimens of this nature have been found to attribute such a phenomenon to small-scale catastrophies. Not only have dinosaurs been found in flood-deposited layers, they have also been found encased in large masses of ironstone material that appears to have fallen from the heavens.

An article called "Dinosaur Bones Lifted From Rocks," taken from the *Saskatoon Star,* August 26, 1981, tells about a dinosaur found near Huxley, Alberta, Canada, that was covered in 80 tons of ironstone. The article states:

> *In addition to the fossil bones, scientists found fossilized imprints of the dinosaur's skin, giving them an idea of the beast's outer appearance. They also discovered and removed a set of fossil footprints, the final tracks that the carnivore left as it died.*

How can the theory of uniformitarianism possibly explain the presence of skin and footprints in the ironstone material? Such evidence can only be logically explained by a sudden destruction and rapid fossilization.

Over the years, numerous theories for the extinction of the dinosaur have been suggested by scientists, attempting to explain their demise by some gradual process. Some believe the reason they died out was because of a gradual change in climatic conditions. Others think that factors like disease and diet could have been the reason.

The most recent theory of dinosaur extinction, proposed by a scientist by the name of Luis Alvarez, suggests that dinosaurs and many other kinds of life were catastrophically destroyed by a cosmic collision of an asteroid or comet with the earth. Since evolutionary geologists have assumed that dinosaurs disappeared 65 million years ago in the past, Alvarez has arrived at a similar date for the cataclysm. The theory of a sudden destruction of the dinosaur kind is based on the discovery of an element of cosmic origin called iridium found in association with dinosaur fossils.

The new theory for the destruction of the dinosaur kind has opened the door for a revision to the evolutionary premise of uniformitarianism. Scientists who are willing to examine some of their preconceived ideas and look at the evidence with an open mind are coming to the conclusion that our earth has been devastated by global destructions of cosmic origin. This agrees completely with what the Bible claims has taken place in the past.

## Frozen Fossils

One of the most astonishing features of the fossil record which confirms life has been destroyed catastrophically in a moment of time are the vast quantities of plants and animals found in a frozen condition. One area where an unbelievable number of plants and animals are found frozen in ice and muck is the Fairbanks region in Alaska. Gold mining operations in this area during the 1940s opened up mile-long cuts in the frozen muck, which revealed the sudden destruction of hundreds of life forms. On page 151 of the book *Early Man In The New World,* the author K. Macgowen makes the following comment about observations of frozen animals at this location:

> *Their numbers are appalling. They lie frozen in tangled masses, interspersed with uprooted trees. They seem to have been torn apart and dismembered and then consolidated under catastrophic conditions. Skin, ligament, hair, flesh can still be seen.*

Along the coastline of Northern Siberia and into Alaska are buried the remains of millions of mammoths. In some places the mammoth bones are so thickly packed together, they make up much of the substance of the soil. In some places the mammoths are entombed in the ice; in other places they are frozen into sedimentary strata. *(Figure 81.)*

*Figure 81:*
*Hundreds of thousands of mammoths have been found frozen in the ice fields of Siberia and Alaska. Early explorers to these regions used the frozen meat from the carcasses of the mammoths to feed their dogs.*

Examination of the carcasses of these great animals reveals they must have been frozen instantly. Food is preserved in their stomachs before the potent digestive juices have had a chance to break it down. Summer vegetation such as grass, bluebells, and buttercups have been found in their mouths. Many of these great beasts have been found torn and ripped apart, frozen in the ice. Camels, sheep, rhinos, bison, horses, and lions have also been embedded in ice in Siberia and Alaska. The overwhelming evidence clearly confirms a scene of catastrophic death involving millions of animals.

No process going on anywhere in the world today is comparable to the events which have entombed countless varieties of life in the past. No process is occurring today which preserves life in a fossilized condition as it certainly has done in the past. The earth's layers reveal millions upon millions of plant and animal remains, often grouped together in what appear to be massive graveyards. Evolutionists are not able to explain these things, for evolution theory rests upon the concept of uniformitarianism. However, the evidence confirms the biblical premise of catastrophic destruction of life on a global basis. What God's Word states has taken place in the past can be backed up and supported by the evidence clearly observed in the world around us.

# EPILOGUE

The major objective in writing this book has been to contrast the two opposing views for the origin and history of life. We have looked at the foundational principles of the creation and the evolution view of origins. We have also looked at evidence which either supports or challenges the basic principles of each model. In light of the evidence presented, we need to ask ourselves the following question. Which model of origins can be supported by the observable evidence?

Each one of us, if we are willing to examine the evidence with an open mind, is personally responsible for making a decision. Which of the two opposing views is true? Depending on views or opinions of others falls short of using our own logic and reasoning ability. The past has proven that relying totally upon the theories of science has led many intelligent people astray. The apostle Paul warned Timothy of the danger of rejecting God and accepting knowledge that is the result of human reasoning. In 1 Timothy 6: 20-21 he wrote, "O Timothy, keep that which is committed to thy trust, avoiding profane and vain babblings, and oppositions of science falsely so called: which some professing have erred concerning the faith."

The human mind has the ability to evaluate information and make decisions based upon facts. The Living Bible states, "Just as my mouth can taste good food, so my mind can taste truth when I hear it" (Job 12:11). Refusing to deal with the facts just because they do not fit with our preconceived ideas is not being honest. A fact that contradicts a man-made theory, even though it agrees with the Bible, is still a fact.

The creation-evolution controversy is important for more than the purpose of establishing an authentic model of origins. The creation view of the origin and history of man is closely tied with an accurate perspective of the spiritual relationship that exists between God and man.

The biblical model clearly teaches that man was created in the image of God. As long as man was obedient to his Creator, a loving and harmonious relationship would have existed for eternity. The human choice to rebel against God brought about the fall, the curse, and the ultimate separation of a Holy God from wicked, sinful, human beings.

The evolution model for the origin and history of man totally rejects the view that man is destined for a lost eternity. In fact, the popular concept at the present time is that human-consciousness is rapidly taking a quantum leap of evolution, ascending to a higher level never before experienced.

The Bible, the key to understanding the early earth, is also the key to understanding the greatest spiritual need of man. The Bible states that Jesus Christ came to this earth and died upon the cross to provide salvation for all those who would believe in this act of redemption. John 3:16 states: ''For God so loved the world, that he gave his only begotten Son, that whosoever believeth in him should not perish, but have everlasting life.''

The gift of eternal life is free, by the grace of God, to all those who make the willful choice to believe in Jesus Christ. Romans 10: 9-10 states: ''If thou shalt confess with thy mouth the Lord Jesus, and shalt believe in thine heart that God hath raised him from the dead, thou shalt be saved. For with the heart man believeth unto righteousness; and with the mouth confession is made unto salvation.''

Have you made that commitment to Jesus Christ? It is our prayer that if you have not, you will do so in the very near future.

# About The Authors

Dr. Glen McLean, Roger Oakland and Larry McLean were involved together as a seminar ministry team that was based at the Full Gospel Bible Institute in Eston, Saskatchewan, Canada from 1980 to 1988. The seminar which they presented throughout Canada and the United States during this period of time was called *The Bible: Key To Understanding Science, History and the Future.*

**Dr. Glen McLean,** senior member of the team, has researched and presented Bible and Science related subjects for over 50 years. He has been a guest on numerous radio and television talk shows and has lectured at many churches, schools, and colleges. Dr. McLean was a pastor and a Bible School president for 39 years, and is currently chancellor of the Full Gospel Bible Institute in Eston, Saskatchewan, Canada.

**Roger Oakland,** a former supporter of the evolutionary world view and a biology instructor, now lectures worldwide on the subject of the creation-evolution controversy and its connection with the New Age movement. Based in southern California since 1988, Roger has founded an international ministry called **Understand The Times** which is dedicated to strengthening the faith of Christians and challenging unbelievers about what they believe. Other books and audiovisual materials which Roger has either produced or co-produced are listed in the catalogue at the back of this book.

**Larry McLean,** Dr. McLean's son, grew up sharing his father's interest in the Bible and science field. Since 1988 he has been based in Vancouver, Canada where he continues to be interested in creation topics as they are related to his involvement with mining exploration. Larry was instrumental in the production of a 14 part video teaching series called *The Bible: Key To Understanding Science, History and the Future.* This series is still available by contacting F.G.B.I., P.O. Box 579, Eston, Saskatchewan Canada SOL 1AO.

Understand The Times, Inc. is a non-profit tax deductible organization and is recognized as such both in the United States and Canada.

Understand The Times, Inc. publishes a news booklet called *Understand The Times*. Its main purpose is to make known intelligent reasons for our Christian faith and to give practical action steps for fulfilling the Great Commission.

Winter 1994 News Booklet

The following books, videos and audio cassettes are made available by the ministry, so that the body of Christ may be strengthened and the ministry goals can be met.

# AUDIO TAPES OF
# THE SIX PART SEMINAR SERIES

## The Evidence For Creation

How and when did life begin? Was it the result of random chance processes over millions of years of time, or was life designed by a Creator?

"The Evidence For Creation" audio tape series examines the fundamental principles of the evolution and creation models and tests them against the observable evidence.

### ( 6 Tape Pack )

---

## Understand The Times

The "Understand The Times" audio tape series is designed to educate people as to what is taking place in the world around us from a biblical perspective. It challenges and equips the listener to be better prepared for the times in which we are living.

### ( 6 Tape Pack )

# DOCUMENTARY VIDEOS

### The Death of the Dinosaur

Dinosaur extinction is a subject that seems to fascinate just about everyone. The fossilized remains of dinosaurs have been found buried in the layers of the earth all over the world. What happened to them? Did they die out gradually, or were they destroyed by a global catastrophe?

The Death of the Dinosaur" examines the mystery of dinosaur extinction by evaluating the observable evidence and comparing it with two opposite world views- creation or evolution.

## *Also available in Russian*

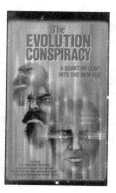

### The Evolution Conspiracy

A fast moving documentary presenting the creation-evolution debate in an appealing format featuring some of the world's most influential experts on both sides of the issue.

# VIDEO LECTURE SERIES

Each of these three one hour long lecture style videos is an ideal teaching tool for use in Christian Schools, Sunday Schools or Home Bible Studies.

### The Evidence For Creation

The subject of origins has been a controversial issue between supporters of the two opposing views - creation and evolution.

This video examines the basic principles of the biblical account and shows how it is supported by the facts of biology and geology.

*Also available in Russian*

### Evolution: Fact or Fiction

Many scientists today claim the evolutionary world view is the only acceptable explanation for the origin and history of life. Other scientists claim that this is not true.

This video examines the foundational principles of the evolutionary model and examines them in light of the observable evidence

### Ancient Man: Created or Evolved

The subject of the origin and history of mankind has triggered heated debate between supporters of the two opposing views - creation and evolution.

This video examines both models and tests them against the evidence found in the fossil record and the remains left by ancient civilizations.

*Also available in Russian*

# BOOKS

### The Evolution Conspiracy

What was once a classroom debate now reaches into every corner of our lives. In this alarming expose, the authors show that the raging war between evolution and creation is not a battle between *science* and religion but a battle between *religion* and religion - with tremendous social, moral and eternal consequences for everyone.

---

### Let There Be Light

Roger Oakland's personal testimony, reveals how God's Holy Spirit is at work in the world today. Written in a biographical style which communicates to everyone, this book charts Roger's spiritual journey from a zealous defender of the theory of evolution to an enthusiastic supporter of the Biblical model of creation. Now his mission is to point people to the light of the gospel of Jesus Christ, by presenting the scientific evidence supporting the existence of the Creator to people around the world.

---

### Understand The Times

This book presents a basic biblical understanding concerning the beliefs, teachings and events sweeping the world today. It is written in an easy to understand format and answers the question: Could we be living in the generation that will witness the return of Jesus Christ for His Church? The reader is challenged to awaken to reality by looking to the Bible for solid insight into what is happening in the world, why these things are happening, and where we are headed in the future.

# MINISTRY INFORMATION

Both *"The Evidence For Creation"* and *"Understand The Times"* books have been translated and published in the Russian language. There are currently over 300,000 copies in circulation.

"The Evidence For Creation" will soon be available in Spanish and Bulgarian. Translations are also underway in Chinese, Japanese and Serbo-Croation.

To order any of the proceeding materials you may call the toll free order desk at:

1 800 689-1888

If you would like to receive a complimentary copy of the latest **" Understand The Times"** newsbooklet you may write to:

Understand The Times
Roger Oakland Ministries
P.O. Box 27239
Santa Ana, CA 92799